Praises for *FROM C*

"Sally speaks to wounded souls suffering from childhood trauma with grace and compassion. She delicately takes readers on a journey saturated with pain and darkness. But while the stories are intense and vulnerable, she offers hope and a safety net to those silently suffering. In a world desperate for clarity and peace, Sally offers a path to redemption and healing. This book is highly relevant and a must read regardless of gender, background or experiences."

~Brendie D. Heter, Author, Public Speaker, MPA

"For anyone who has felt alone or has lost hope of their lives ever improving, this book is a must. The traumas faced by Naomi changed how she felt about herself and about her ability to influence the world around her. It is in moving past negative self-talk and destructive behavior that Naomi is enabled to forgive herself, allowing her to connect more genuinely with those around her. This is a book about hope and how to become the best version of your true self."

~Deborah Silverman, PhD, Licensed Psychologist

"Sally Betters tells a story so heartbreakingly beautiful and so painful to comprehend—one wants to look away and keep reading all at the same time. *From Crisis to Compassion* draws one in and is brimming with Scriptural truth and the deep, unstoppable, Redemptive love of Christ, bringing healing to those who have suffered in secret and silence. In a unique style and voice, Sally writes with a grit and compassion that could only come from a personal encounter with a passionate Savior who will stop at nothing to rescue His beloved."

~Susan Vandepol, Author of Life after Breath

"Grief is cumulative and cumulatively negative. Childhood abuse can have a lifelong negative impact on your life. *From Crisis to Compassion* is a beautiful example of how hope and recovery from grief and abuse are possible."

~*Gina Thompson, Certified Grief Recovery Specialist*

"The term 'broken heart' is so commonly used in our society that it often sounds romantic; and in actuality it's anything but! Broken hearts demand our full attention, whether the cause is relationships, debilitating depression, or dreams dying and crumbling in our hands, we are all in need of healing from the heart traumas of simply being human.

Sally is passionate not only for her own healing but making it accessible for others as well. Within the narrative on these pages you'll find your story... follow the path and you'll find your healing."

~*Marty Walker, Lead Pastor, The Sanctuary Church, Santa Clarita, CA*

"This book is a powerful testimony to the faithfulness of God to those of us who have suffered at the hands of others. His faithfulness to protect, provide and redeem is evidenced throughout this well written and compelling story. A must read!"

~*Carole Boersma, President, Restored through Christ Ministries*

"I have never heard a story of someone healing or getting over something by living in silence and isolation with past abuse. I am grateful for this example of transparency, honesty, and bravery in telling a story out loud. This book can serve as a guide for anyone who wants to come out spiritually and relationally stronger after sexual abuse or abortion. Thank you Sally, for writing the truth!"

~*Wendy McHaddad, Spiritual Care Assistant, Grace Baptist*

FROM CRISIS TO COMPASSION

How to find *Empathy*, *Intimate Connection*, and *Involvement* with *Supportive Community*

SALLY BETTERS

From Crisis to Compassion
How to Find Empathy, Intimate Connection,
and Involvement with Supportive Community
All Rights Reserved
Copyright © 2018 Sally Betters
v 3.0

Scripture in From Crisis to Compassion is taken from the HOLY BIBLE, NEW INTERNATIONAL VERSION, NIV Copyright 1973,1978, 1984, 2011 by Biblica, Inc. unless otherwise indicated.

Published by Author Academy Elite
P.O. Box 43, Powell, Ohio 43065
www.AuthorAcademyElite.com

PRINTED IN THE UNITED STATES OF AMERICA

ISBN: 978-1-64085-339-3 paperback
ISBN: 978-1-64085-340-9 hardcover
ISBN: 978-1-64085-341-6 eBook
Library of Congress Control Number: 2018907289

Cover Design by:
Virtually Possible Designs

Interior Design by:
Jetlaunch

Back Cover Photo:
John Caprarelli

This book is dedicated to the valuable readers who have suffered childhood trauma, a learning disability, an abortion, a miscarriage, or an abusive relationship, I'm so grateful that you picked up this book.

I believe there is one who knows you intimately and desires to draw you close, heal your wounds, and cleanse you from your doubts. He can soothe your heartache and replace it with a deep satisfaction that only He can provide. You can be free from old patterns that hold you back as you step forward into His loving arms.

May you come to know the magnificent love of the Father who romances you through His creation, His word, and His eternal love for you. May you experience his strong arms around you, His amazing forgiveness and His incredible joy that you are His.

I'm praying for restorative opportunities, intimate connection, and a supportive community in your life. You are valuable, worthy, and loved! You were designed to live fully alive!

God often uses our
deepest *pain*
as the launching pad
of our greatest *calling*.

—Beyond Ordinary

CONTENTS

FOREWORD

As you read this book, you'll witness that an invisible war is being waged between seductive evil and unfathomable good. This is truly a compelling story of redemption that takes place over a prolonged period of time. Real truth stands on its own. It's not open for debate, nor can it be negotiated as some may think. Redemption is truth displayed to its fullest extent.

This story is one woman's turbulent struggle with life. Honestly, it's all our story. Where does the courage to face this crisis come from? How can compassion come from this kind of devastation?

It's not something we can wave a magic wand at and it just happens. We are all caught up in our own pain to get past our own crisis. Something or someone needs to act on our behalf in order for real compassion to be expressed and demonstrated. Not just for the short term or the immediate challenge at hand.

How does a child handle the heartbreak of shattered innocence as it jolts her to the core like a bolt of lightning? From early childhood, a young girl willingly envelops a deep secret protecting her loved ones. The fear of rejection, abandonment, and exposure of the truth nips at her heels like a beast out of control.

As you become immersed in Naomi's life from childhood to adulthood, the venomous poison of self-doubt raises its ugly head. To make matters worse, an undiagnosed learning disability and deceptive relationships mount a barrage of deep disappointments. Now one secret turns to many in a constant effort to avoid exposure. A log jam of emotions and fear begin to pile up. Ways of avoiding exposure are consuming her mental energy.

In the midst of all this, Naomi becomes acutely aware that a merciless enemy is tracking her every move. Not seen, but the carnage left behind is becoming evident. Alone in all of this, she is fast losing all hope. Does anyone else know what's going on? Who can she trust?

Author Sally Betters dares to enter into these secret places of darkness and deception. She unveils cultural lies and societal pressures that twist our thinking. Sally shows through her vulnerability in writing and an intimate relationship with our Lord Jesus Christ, life can turn from crisis to compassion.

Kary Oberbrunner, author of *Your Secret Name, The Deeper Path,* and *Day Job to Dream Job*

ACKNOWLEDGEMENTS

First and foremost, I want to honor my Heavenly Father, your only Son, Jesus Christ, and your powerful Holy Spirit. Thank you for your daily presence and deep love for me. You alone are the lifter of my head. The hope you have given me has been the beacon of light that directs my path.

I wish to thank my greatest encourager, my husband and best friend, Richard. You have been my steadfast promoter through so many challenges. The best public relations agent anyone could ask for. You have watched the Lord chisel and define me over the years so I could fulfill His call on my life.

To my parents, two pillars who provided love, a strong work ethic, encouragement and the vision of what could be.

For my sister Norma, thank you for the memories and the laughter.

For my sister and dear friend, Arcy. You have been my lifelong cheerleader, travel partner, confidant and prayer warrior. You and Eddie have given of your time, talents and treasures to richly bless me and my family. Thank you!

For Ryan and Angelo, you are two of my greatest gifts in this life. Thank you for your handsome smiles, engaging laughter, thoughtfulness, insight and love. I am so proud of the young men that you are. I'm forever grateful to have been given the joy of being your Mom. May my ceiling be your floor.

To Elizabeth, my daughter in love. Thank you for your kind encouragement, technical savvy, and sweet love that blesses me.

To my four amazing granddaughters, Oliviana, Alexandra, Kennedy, and Eliana, I'm blessed by your smiles, hugs, drawings, giggles and love. May this world be a better place because of your kindness, joy and love for others.

To the tribe of women who have walked with me along this journey of life. You have made a difference; your words of encouragement, listening ears, friendship, your prayers, your time—all invaluable. It is my great joy to call you friends.

For Pastor Marty Walker, who stepped out of the box to encourage, bless and motivate his congregation to THRIVE. Because of your innovative ways, I can look at worship and living in community in a new light. Thank you.

INTRODUCTION

Stories are powerful. They offer deep revelation and insight. Stories stir our souls, and they help us to live out truth. If we are willing, they can open our eyes and unplug our ears by removing the blinders with which we've grown comfortable. Stories can move us to take action, feel grief and compassion for others, fill us with hope and understanding, and show us how to live deeper lives of compassion with those around us.

Reading this courageous, yet agonizing, story reveals how early childhood experiences shape us as well as impact our decision making as adults. These traumatic experiences alter our self-perception and the intentions of those in whom we place our trust. They impact how we relate to others and how successful—or fatal—our love relationships will be. Without proper education and healing, we are likely to repeat the unhealthy patterns we learned growing up. Additionally, it will directly affect how we raise our own children, thus repeating the cycle.

The history of Naomi Parker is one such narration. Her story was kept hidden for years to protect others from pain and heartache. The irony is that it caused a canyon of despair to grow wider, causing agony and confusion to the very one who desired to shelter others. In this instance, silence was used to insulate the truth, but it continued to snowball and created an avalanche.

This is a colossal story. Naomi lived in the face of shame and deception. It is also a story of redemption and healing filled with life-defining moments—any of which could send someone spiraling into self-pity, depression, drugs, self-injury, or promiscuity. But instead, over time, there was a multi-layer of reconciliation between God, those who wounded Naomi Parker, and those she hurt.

Naomi's transparent account of her life can easily represent women and men everywhere. With candid, unmasked reflection of life events, she removes the veil of cultural lies and deception. Given the statistics of childhood molestation, learning disabilities, abortion, miscarriage, and abusive marriages, her relevant story has similarly played out in the lives of others. If you look around, it easily represents more than half the population of the United States of America. The numbers might be larger in other countries with varying cultural traditions and repressive laws.

You may have experienced many of the life-changing traumas revealed in this book and are searching for answers. You may have thought that you were the only one who felt this way. Maybe you have tentatively reached out to others for comfort and understanding only to be left wanting. Friends and family, although well intended, could have caused deeper pain and heartache by telling you how you should feel or what you should have done differently. Rarely can someone who is untrained be fully capable of understanding the profound craters you've navigated and the scars you've hidden from public view. But evidence of this devastation will surface in your choices at every level.

The intention of writing Naomi Parker's story is to reveal the cultural lies, unhealthy talk-tracks, and destructive behaviors and to begin to move you to a place of sharing your own hurt within a safe and appropriate community. You may be led to forgive and find healing through giving back to those who also need help. It is in this type of healthy community that you will find caring, sincere, and genuine individuals who desire to connect with you.

Whatever road you have walked and whatever baggage you carry, I invite you to step with me into this woman's life. Experience the emotions of fear, shame, confusion, and deception so that you may come away with great hope. May you also be convinced of the overwhelming love of our Father God through His powerful promises and assurance of His presence during this difficult journey.

"Hope deferred makes the heart sick, but a longing fulfilled is a tree of life" (Proverbs 13:12).

My prayer is that you will clearly see God's hand of intervention in Naomi's specific circumstances. Within these pages, you will find great hope in His Word, provision in the practical daily needs for Naomi and her sons, and protection from the evil that entered her life at various stages of her development.

Most importantly, I hope that you will see that Naomi's story as part of a larger story. It's an all too common narrative of life in our fallen world. It is a turbulent world of unrelenting changes where we face the gaping jaws of uncertainty. Here, in this unstable world, there is a vicious enemy whose time is short. He has no regard for the value of life, innocence of children, or those who suffer at the hand of another. His daily focus is to kill our dreams, steal our hope, and destroy any joy we have in the goodness of our God. But this epic story also has a great Liberator who gives us direct access to Himself. He is our protector, provider, encourager, and guide. He never runs out of resources, has an unlimited capacity to bless us, and gives us a foretaste of what we will experience eternally with Him in Heaven. The choice is left with us to trust Him.

"For our struggle is not against flesh and blood, but against the rulers, against the powers, against the world forces of this darkness, against the spiritual forces of wickedness in the heavenly places" (Ephesians 6:12, NASB).

1

THE SECRETS

Every experience God gives us, every person he puts in our lives is the perfect preparation for the future only He can see.

—Corrie Ten Boom[1]

This is the life story of Naomi Parker. It is told from her perspective …

I am the youngest of three girls born into a Hispanic family during the 1950's. We were raised by caring and hardworking parents who did their best to provide for us. They raised us to be honorable, respectable girls. We dutifully worked alongside each other at home and at our family restaurant.

As early as seven years of age, my mother picked up my sisters and me after school and took us to serve at our restaurant. There we worked together waiting on customers, preparing orders, washing dishes, and doing our homework. I worked in the back-kitchen chopping lettuce, tomatoes, onions, and grating large chunks of cheese for tacos, burritos, and burgers. Nothing came pre-grated in those days. My sisters were old enough to be out front with the public and served as waitresses. They were cute and petite and wore crisp, white, uniforms like my mother.

Peeling large boxes of hot chilis to make my mother's signature salsa was a job I dreaded. Invariably, I would touch my eyes, nose, or mouth without thinking and start crying from the fire-hot sting that lit me up like a firecracker. My dad had a simple trick to remove the sting. He would take a piece of my long, dark hair and rub it over my sizzling skin. The oil from my hair would absorb the heat on my skin, and the fire would cease. It was an old-fashioned remedy that worked, and I was grateful for it.

Our restaurant was located in a strip-mall in a quiet suburb of Southern California. Tucked between a Chinese food restaurant and a dry cleaner, we served up traditional Mexican food and hamburgers with friendly customer service. All ingredients were fresh and meals were made to order. My parents didn't know how to skimp on quality, so they delivered a huge value for a meager cost. Their financial profits were slim with the growing competition of fast food taco stands sprouting up around us.

The large glass cabinets in the front of our restaurant held beautifully carved onyx chess sets, paperweights, and wooden marionette puppets. My Uncle Jack had an import-export business and was able to get a reduced price for the items my parents desired to sell. Near the cash register was an old, red soda machine that had *Coca-Cola* written on it in white letters. Next to the sodas were boxes of candies for sale: red and black licorice, Abba Zabbas, Hershey bars, Cup of Golds, and Butterfingers. These became a treasure chest for my potential financial rewards and emotional appeasement.

From the age of seven until I was around thirteen, reloading the soda machine and managing the candy counter was my department. I was the seller of candies to all the neighborhood kids who came into our restaurant. As the youngest family member doing business with the community, this job gave me a sense of responsibility and control. Since I couldn't wait tables and receive tips like my older sisters, this was my domain. My dad would give me a percentage of what I sold at the end of the day. Hearing coins jingle in my pocket was a thrill. I tried hard to be the best candy salesperson I could be.

For as long as I can remember, my father always worked two jobs. He left his first manual labor job as a mattress maker exhausted. He would then drive for over an hour to our restaurant. Once there, he walked in with a smile on his face, kissed my mother, and hugged my sisters and me. Then my father would quickly clean up, put on a white shirt, wrap a white apron around his waist, and work his second job of washing dishes and waiting on tables. If business was slow, he would send my mother and older sisters' home so they could complete household chores and prepare for work and school the next day.

Given a choice, I always chose to stay at the restaurant with my dad. Together we washed all the dishes, swept the floors, stacked the chairs, and mopped the store from back to front. We took pride in leaving the place sparkling clean for my mom to enjoy when she opened it up the next morning.

Turning around the sign in our store window to the closed/ cerrado side was my symbolic way of putting another day behind me. This was a special time with my dad. I treasured his joyful personality and the one-on-one conversations we had. His positive attitude was welcoming and complimented his handsome smile.

I looked up to my father and my mother. They could do anything in my eyes. They were my heroes. It was evident that they were never afraid to work hard to support us. I appreciated their determination to run a family business with less than a high school education. Without formal or business training, they persevered to produce quality food at a time when fast-food corporations were swallowing up small, family-owned restaurants. These two pillars were my role models, and I never wanted to disappoint them.

One of our primary family values was loyalty. This was demonstrated in various ways. Sometimes it was taking in wayward family members—supporting those without work or who had marital problems or teenage rebellion in their homes. Also, regularly visiting grandparents, aunts, uncles, and cousins was part of our traditional culture. We never went anywhere empty handed. We always had a bag of pan dulce (Mexican sweet bread), and something tasty my mother had made to share with our loved ones. My parents were loving, kind people who never betrayed their family no matter what.

Before continuing, may I share this: I am not an expert in any of the challenges I am about to share with you. Rather, I see myself as a mere reflector of the grace and love of my faithful Heavenly Father. Each facet I am privileged to reflect here is a result of being molded and chiseled, through my trials, so I may radiate more of His character. Any sparkle you may see in this story is a direct refining of His grace and goodness in my life.

We lived on a double lot in East Los Angeles, California, with a small back-house behind us. That was where my Aunt Barbara and Uncle Vick lived. They rented the back-house from my parents. This was my mother's favorite sister. Aunt Barbara had raised her, and their love ran deep. Our families spent a lot of time together around the kitchen table for birthdays, holidays, and just doing life. My mom and Aunt Barbara were inseparable.

My aunt was a very hard-working woman, like my mother. She would get up at 4 a.m. every morning to make a hearty breakfast for my uncle and prepare him a fresh lunch before he left for work. Then, to earn a few dollars, Aunt Barbara would stand for hours ironing clothes for other people. She was the salt-of-the-earth—loyal, kind, and loving. She was like a grandmother to me, and I loved her dearly.

Every birthday, Aunt Barbara brought me a beautifully-wrapped box filled with something she had made or bought with her hard-earned money. Every Christmas, she knit my sisters and me slippers to keep us warm. She was a dutiful wife, mother, sister, and aunt. Her contented laugh brought joy into our discussions. Aunt Barbara always dressed nicely with clean, crisp clothes, accented with matching earrings and a dab of perfume. I enjoyed her self-taught talents and her endearing smile.

Uncle Vick and Aunt Barbara's daughter and son were unusually polite and equally as pristine with their clothing. To look at their family was like picking up a Hallmark card: a handsome father and mother, one girl and one boy, well dressed, well-mannered, and every hair in place. From the outside, they looked like the perfect family. But what went on behind closed doors was a different story.

The confusing tragedy is that my uncle was an alcoholic who sexually abused me for several years. He told me I was special, and this was our little secret. Because he loved me, he wanted to be near me. He told me I was his favorite of all his nieces, and there was something special about me that made him want to be close to me. "This is our little secret," he said. And I must never tell.

Since they lived behind us for the first few years of my life, I don't know exactly when the abuse began. My mother told me that my Aunt Barbara and Uncle Vick used to take care of me when she went to work. It wasn't unusual for my aunt to leave the room to hang clothes, prepare a meal, or take care of her personal needs. The tender boundaries of my innocence were shattered, and the emotional fractures from his assault would grow deeper as time went on.

Frequently, our large extended family would gather at the home of my maternal grandparents to celebrate holidays or birthdays. Conversations were loud and food was plentiful. I would hang out with my cousins both inside the house and out in my Grandmother Sonya's beautiful garden. She spent many hours tilling the ground and could grow anything. Everyone loved her fragrant herbs, colorful array of flowers, and the well-cared-for garden that was framed with fruit trees.

My Grandfather Joseph, was a talented carpenter and built patio tables and chairs to accentuate my grandma's green thumb. Their skills were an asset to their large family. My grandparents had eleven children, six sons and five daughters, who would come to visit with their children, totaling about 35 grandchildren at the time. Although, not all of them attended every family gathering, there were always a lot of people around.

The freedom of playing and acting like a child eluded me because my eye was always on my Uncle Vick. I was careful not to be alone in a room when he was near. Keeping a healthy distance, or standing close to someone safe was a constant priority. Watching him was my preoccupation. I looked for nonverbal clues of his body language and the tone of his voice to anticipate his next move. This tiring visual detection along with the emotional anxiety robbed me of being able to roam freely and enjoy the celebrations at my grandparents' home.

One time, as evening drew near, I saw my Uncle Vick carefully sneak out of my grandparents' house. I watched him through an opening in the backyard gate, camouflaging myself behind a prickly rosebush. He slid in on the passenger side of his car, opened the glove box, and pulled out a small, brown bag. He brought it up to his mouth and swung his head back. Inside that bag was a pocket-sized whiskey bottle. He had them stashed in convenient places, so he could cope with whatever demons plagued his soul.

After a few more swigs, Uncle Vick climbed out of his car and staggered back into my grandparents' house with a half-cocked smile on his face and the smell of liquor on his breath. Looking over his shoulder, he shoved the brown bag in his jacket. He had found his courage through the numbing liquid that flooded his veins.

Although I didn't understand the magnitude of his drinking problem, I knew it made it easier for him to look for me in the family crowd. I dodged him at every turn and stressed over being within his reach. I didn't want to be near Uncle Vick so he could reach out to caress my cheek or stroke my back. Although this would seem innocent and acceptable among our affectionate family, I knew his true intentions.

His pathetic voice, slumped shoulders, and the way he looked for meaning at the bottom of a whiskey bottle repulsed me. I didn't respect him and only tolerated Uncle Vick's presence because I had to. At a young age, there was so much I didn't understand. I worked hard not to create any problems that would draw attention to myself by anyone in the family.

One afternoon while standing in the kitchen anxiously watching my mother cook, I finally got the courage to tell her my secret. I must have been around eight or nine years old. She questioned what I was doing that would "invite" such behavior. I knew revealing the sordid details would change the relationship between my mother and Aunt Barbara. I would be to blame. It would also change the relationship between my aunt and me. The thought of that rejection from those I loved was emotionally crippling. Bringing this to my parents' attention was a no-win situation.

It took a great deal of courage for me to broach this subject with my mother. But after hearing her accusatory reaction, I felt forced to bury the secret even further. She never asked me about it again.

To prepare for family visits, I would stand in our kitchen popping sugar cubes in my mouth, trying to control my anxiety, before my Aunt Barbara and Uncle Vick walked through the door. Those white cubes were my ticket to deeper breathing and a pleasant rush to calm my racing heart. It was a way to anesthetize myself from the fear, anger, and confusion that rushed through my veins. Sugar had become my addictive drug of choice. As a young child, it seemed to calm my anxiety—for the moment. Little did I know, this long-term addiction of sugar would be as strong as cocaine and equally as hard to break away from. This would eventually cause health issues and become a regular reflex for comfort.

Culturally, there was no respect or trust from the voice of a child. We were literally given the message to be seen but not heard. Never was our opinion or input welcomed in adult circles. We were looked at as an ornament if we were good and a nuisance if we didn't obey. This was an accepted way of relating to children when I was growing up, so it didn't seem to be wrong. At that time, and for decades later, I had no voice. Later, I would see how this abuse would alter *all* my decision making.

To stay busy, as I entered high school, I participated in student government and ran for various offices. The distraction from the negative self-talk coiling through my mind was a welcomed change. I enjoyed feeling like I could earn the approval of others. My drive to become someone respected and knowledgeable took priority over my shattered heart. The busier I remained, the less I had time to feel.

My Uncle Vick's abuse continued until my sophomore year in high school. He went from sexually abusing me to telling me how proud he was of my accomplishments. He made it a point to do this in front of my parents or my aunt so it would seem complementary. He watched me from afar and saw how hard I pushed myself at school. He would always comment on any awards I received and acted like he cared about me. I wondered if he was truly sorry for the indelible harm he had caused in my life. Unfortunately, he never apologized.

When I was still living at home with my parents, my Aunt Barbara came to live with us. My Uncle Vick had hit her, and her face was bruised. Years of verbal, emotional, and physical abuse had taken their toll, and my aunt was defeated, tired, and unable to cope. My mother had asked her to come and stay with us so she could regain her emotional and physical strength.

My Aunt Barbara had endured this crazy abusive cycle for as long as she could. Initially, she had wanted to remain in their home to protect her children from the scary verbal, physical, and sexual assault that had grown like cancer in their home. Later on, she stayed because she had no skills to support herself. Her life was anything but what she had hoped for. The false public presentation had continued for too long. Now she bore the physical, emotional, and mental scars of living with an abuser.

My heart ached to see my Aunt Barbara, now in her older years, struggling to find her confidence. She looked so defeated. I had mixed emotions seeing the extent of damage the years of being married to an alcoholic had done to her. A large part of me was boiling with rage. The other part was angry with my aunt for not taking a stand and separating from him when the problems started early in her marriage. But as I mentioned earlier, *loyalty* was the norm no matter what the cost—even at the expense of truth. I often wondered if Aunt Barbara had been stronger and demanded Uncle Vick leave years ago, would I have had to endure all those years of his ugly, disgusting, advances towards me?

In retrospect, I wonder what my aunt's life could have been if she had been free to share the shame of her abusive marriage among her family. What if Aunt Barbara had the courage and support to step outside of her cultural script—a script that kept her captive? Maybe if she had received quality counseling about the characteristics of an abuser, she might have escaped from that cycle of torture. What if she would have had a supportive community around her that offered a way to take the needed steps to remove herself, and her children, from the degrading tirade of verbal and physical assault? What would Aunt Barbara's life have looked like with regular encouragement and support?

I didn't know about marriage, at that time, and how distorted a relationship with an abuser could be. But these questions floated in and out of my mind when I was around her: How had she lost her focus of what love was supposed to look like? When did her dreams of having a respectable husband and father to her children vanish over the years? Why had she decided to accept her role as an abused wife? Why didn't she leave sooner and give herself a chance to start over? This hideous expression of *loyalty* was suffocating. It destroyed lives like a venomous poison. Never did I think I would someday ask myself the same questions.

Years later, my Uncle Vick would become diagnosed with cirrhosis of the liver, and it would eventually claim his life. I remember standing, dry-eyed, at his bedside with my mother, Aunt Barbara, and a cousin as they tearfully said their good-byes in that stark hospital room. Glancing around his bed, I looked at each person standing there crying and telling him nice things that weren't true. I said nothing.

His hospital room had a sterile smell, like rubbing alcohol. Everything was white: the walls, sheets, medical equipment, and even the nurses' uniforms. What a contrast! There was a purity around us antithetical to the life he lived. The smell of rubbing alcohol permeated my nostrils. It was a different kind of alcohol than my uncle was used to; this type was used to sterilize and kill germs, unlike the alcohol he consumed every day that poisoned his body.

Uncle Vick was dying, and I was secretly thankful. Finally, on that day, I unrealistically believed my secret would die with him. I believed I would never have to reveal the ugly truth of his pathetic words in my ears and his vulgar advances toward me. This was not the case, and the secret grew larger inside of my mind as the years went by. Looking back, I can see the symptoms of abuse from as early as three to four years of age: shame, anxiety, lack of self-esteem, self-hatred, disempowerment, overeating, teeth grinding, and a desire to control my surroundings—all in an effort to manage the chaos within me.

My internal conflict and anxiety manifested in teeth grinding from the tension and fear I held in my young body. This eventually would lead to Temporomandibular Joint Disorder (TMJ), a painful condition of the jaw which can be caused by teeth clenching, grinding, and stress. Since I could not verbalize my secret, it remained locked inside me, and I clenched my jaw to keep it hidden. All I knew was that this terrible feeling inside must have been my fault, and I could not share it with anyone. Why would I want someone else to hear this torrent of emotional pain and feel as badly as I did? I was convinced this was a secret blot on my life. It would be carried to the grave with me.

The impact of this devastating, hidden part of me was like a grenade waiting to go off inside my heart. Like any untreated problem, this destructive secret grew bigger as the years went by. The damage to my heart and soul had been seared into me. Sometimes I would be so angry and enraged that I didn't understand where it came from. It could be triggered from a movie, a conversation about human trafficking or abuse of children, or a news broadcast. Wrestling with this emotion brought confusion over my inability to be content and satisfied. I wanted to be happy with the life I had been given, but contentment escaped me.

School was very difficult and provided an added daily stress. This was due to an undiagnosed learning disability. It was an unwelcomed addition to my already confused mental process. My invisible barrier compounded the academic struggles of mentally processing information, reading, comprehension, and written expression. With this albatross around my neck, all my years of formal education would be grueling. It seemed like nothing was easy for me. I didn't see that I had any talent in any area of my life. I wondered if I would ever make a contribution like other kids who appeared to be smart.

My teachers frequently asked me if I was reading ahead. When given a short class assignment, I was the only one still reading after the allotted time had ended. The truth was, I struggled to finish the brief reading assignment given to the class. Reading was an unconquered battleground for me. The words often ran together, and I would forget them as quickly as I read them. My mind felt like a sieve; everything just ran through and didn't stick.

Comprehension was almost nonexistent. I read the same paragraph over and over, trying to determine what it was saying to me. My frustration grew, and I didn't understand why I couldn't unlock the mystery of reading and remembering what I had read. It was a constant mental cycle of feeling dumb, hopeless, and helpless. There was definitely a block that stemmed from both the learning disability and the emotional conflict that always raged from within.

No matter how hard I tried, I couldn't manage to read and write like everyone else. The thoughts were always circling in my head, but they never came out as quickly, or articulately, as when I listened to other people. Frustration and hopelessness grew within me, and I turned to food for comfort. After dinner, while cleaning up the kitchen, I would pick at the left-overs but never seemed satisfied. The insatiable hunger that silently growled within my depths only made matters worse. Sneaking food to my room was not unusual after making school lunches for my sisters and me. It was a welcomed treat to sedate myself to sleep and had become my way to cope with feeling badly. I was growing bigger on the outside while my secret grew larger on the inside.

I recall a dismal visit to Sears with my mom to buy school clothes. We took several stylish items to the dressing room, and she sat there as I tried on numerous outfits. Nothing fit properly. After going back several times to get larger sizes, she grew frustrated. My mother told me she was disgusted with the amount of weight I had gained. She said, "That's it! You need to go on a diet." We walked to the car without purchasing any clothes for school. I walked behind her sniffling and feeling like I was such a big disappointment. It seemed like I just couldn't do anything right. She didn't know that I ate to suppress the secret monster that growled within me. I knew I could never tell her.

One fateful day, the school nurse came into our sixth-grade classroom with a large hospital-looking scale. Each student was called up in alphabetical order to the front of the class to get weighed and measured. I gripped my chair as I sat at the back of the class, feeling terrified as I heard the nurse call out each person's weight in a loud voice for my teacher to record. Was there no mercy? My goodness, couldn't she at least whisper? Who cared what everyone weighed anyway? I wanted to run out and hide in the girls' bathroom and pretend I had to vomit. But before I could bolt out of the classroom, my name was called. My stomach turned like a merry-go-round as I walked to the front of the class. Everyone heard a thud as I stepped on the scale. The nurse kept moving the silver metal marker to the right to get the scale to balance. When it finally came to a stop she looked at me with a stunned expression on her face, and my eyes grew big and welled up with tears. I'm sure she could see the terror in my eyes. Mercy must have been in the room that day. She leaned over and whispered my weight to my teacher, rather than shouting it out like she did with all the other small, normal-sized kids.

During parent-teacher conferences, my teachers would tell my mother that I was a nice girl but was the slowest reader in the class. The possibility of me going on to college, if I graduated from high school, was not very hopeful. Numerous instructors told both my mother and me that I simply needed to just try harder. The struggle was real. Processing information seemed to go in slow motion and it became more apparent as my classes got harder.

While growing up I would listen to my sister, Rebecca, summarize a movie or program we watched together. I was secretly amazed by how she could clearly organize her thoughts. She was chronologically accurate and concise with the details. Conversely, when I tried to retell a movie or explain something I had experienced, I would get lost with the sequence and become confused. The puzzled look on the faces of my audience would tell me to stop trying.

Years later, while taking post-graduate level classes on children with learning disabilities, I learned that sexual and emotional trauma can make processing any information extremely difficult. This is compounded even more when faced with a learning disability.

My life was filled with confusion and loneliness. There was an ugly, dark secret I carried. It circled through my mind with feelings of shame and guilt. My efforts to control the internal turmoil resulted in constant overeating to change the way I looked. My underlying thought was, I must be doing something wrong with my body to attract this kind of degrading attention. So it made sense to me that if I changed my body, I would not be attractive to anyone. The extra weight was like an armor to protect me from other predators. Unfortunately, it didn't work. We lived next door to a family of three boys, two of which had their turn sexually abusing me. Later, it would include two high school teachers.

I felt like I didn't have an accurate gauge of who I could trust. Even though both my teachers had shown an interest in my activities in Student Government and appeared to be genuine, they ultimately had ulterior motives. The respect I held for each one became tainted after being seduced by them. I was horrified at their brazen advances and verbal seduction. Another wound had lanced my heart and eroded my trust toward men.

During my junior year of high school, I fell in love with a young man named Sam. We were inseparable and dated for three years with plans for marriage. We attended every high school event together and shared holidays with our families. My parents and family adored him and were excited to see what our future held. I honestly felt that he was the son my parents always wanted. He was polite, kind, and respectful. It was a sweet time of feeling genuinely loved and appreciated. Our future looked bright and promising with mutual goals of college, marriage, and a family.

Shortly after high school graduation, while attending college classes, I became pregnant. Once again, I was afraid to confide in my parents for fear of rejection and bringing shame to my family. The pain of disapproval and emotional abandonment was too much for me to bear. It would echo the daily thoughts I carried. Although not in line with our time-frame, I was sure my pregnancy would not be a problem since Sam and I had discussed plans to marry. After I told him about the pregnancy, he shocked me by telling me he wasn't ready for marriage. Within the next few days, he quickly provided the money for an abortion, and he made arrangements at a local abortion facility.

Sam told me he would pick me up on the morning of my appointment like it was any other day we would spend together. There was to be no hint of anything unusual that day. He wanted me to be sure that no one suspected anything that could interfere with his plan. It was a quiet drive to the abortion clinic on that Saturday morning. We were both scared. Sam nervously bit his fingernails as he sat next to me. I carefully filled out the forms.

When they called my name, it was time for me to go back with the nurse. Sam soberly said he would be there waiting when I was done. There were several steps of preparation. First, a young woman explained *the procedure.* She told me I could expect some cramping and bleeding afterwards. I'd be expected to come back for a check-up in a few weeks. Life was supposed to go on like nothing happened.

I felt like I was literally carrying the total responsibility of our intimacy. Sam told me he was going to get some breakfast during the long wait of the abortion. I remember thinking, "How can you eat anything right now?" He still only had to worry about his own physical needs for food. He did not have to go through the grueling torment of having human cells sucked out of his body. After all, this was his idea—for his comfort—because he wasn't ready to have his life disrupted with a child.

This *group of cells* inside of me would be gone, and I would have no worries of an unplanned pregnancy. Nothing was ever mentioned about the years of crushing guilt, shame, and regret this single action would cause. No one talked about the post-abortion symptoms of depression, guilt, anxiety, numbing, sadness, loneliness, depression, anger, nightmares, self-hatred, alcohol/drugs, promiscuity, sleep disorders, hopelessness, anniversary syndrome, abortion flashbacks, eating disorders, self-punishing behavior, or the stages of grief. It was called *a procedure*. There was no mention that the success of this *procedure* meant two people were going into it, but only one would come out alive.

I remember putting on the surgical gown and getting on the operating table. My thoughts raced around in horror wondering what my parents and family would think if they knew what I was doing. Feeling desperate, I dreamed someone would walk through the door of my dressing room to tell me I didn't have to do this; that I would not be judged for having a baby out of wedlock; that I would be supported as I raised this child; that I was valuable; and, even that I could still pursue my dreams of marriage, family, and a career, despite my current out-of-wedlock pregnancy.

Nervously, I waited for my turn to be rolled into the operating room. When they took me in, I saw a doctor dressed in scrubs. Nurses were standing there wearing gloves and looking impatient. I began to cry, and quickly an oxygen mask with a general anesthesia was placed over my face. I don't remember anything until I woke up with blood on my gown, horrible cramps and nausea. Shortly after calling for a nurse, I was asked to sign more forms. Then I was told it was time to leave. "You need to pull yourself together and get dressed," I said to myself. They had several other young women waiting for my bed.

Slowly, I got dressed and met Sam in the waiting room. He nodded to me as if asking, "Is the problem gone?" We walked out silently, two disconnected people who were on a different life trajectory now. I felt empty inside. More than a baby had left my body and my heart. We didn't talk much on the way back to my house. The weight of all this was overwhelming. I felt all alone.

He told me to tell my parents that we had gone out to eat and seen a movie. He picked something he had already seen so he could tell me about it in case they asked me. The world had turned to black and white. I couldn't see the beautiful colors around me anymore.

Sam didn't offer any comfort for what I had just experienced. He seemed to be more relieved that we had dealt with *the problem*, and he didn't have to think about it any longer. I had hoped for some compassion from him about the emotional and physical changes I had experienced over the last few months, not to mention the stress of hiding my nausea at work and at home.

Initially, during the first couple of months after the abortion, there was relief that this *inconvenience* was gone. I was looking forward to getting back to our plans and dreams of getting married and completing our goals in life together. Desperately, I needed some hope to hang onto. But a few months later, Sam became distant and showed less interest in me. He was struggling with his own inner turmoil. He was no longer attentive with phone calls, cards, or wanting to go out or spend time together.

My fear of losing him and our plans for marriage was devastating. Sadness flooded my heart. The joy of life had faded. Sometimes it felt like there was an elephant on my chest and I could barely breathe. Not long afterwards, Sam told me he wanted to date other people. I was crushed, but I tried hard to not show this to my parents. They wondered why we were breaking up. Within a few months, he found someone else he was dating exclusively.

Shame and abandonment covered me all over again. This became another dark secret, and I feared, once more, the disapproval and rejection by the people I loved. I couldn't bear the thought of telling my parents the real reason for our breakup. Hearing their horror and disappointment would be too much to bear. The clouds of loving memories and personal defeat weighed heavily on my mind and overshadowed my hope of getting past the deep heartbreak.

There were huge cultural implications of the shame my secrets would bring to my family: the stigma of an unwed mother and sex outside of marriage. The illusion I clung to of a healthy and safe family became more valued than the truth. The pain that screamed within me was growing louder. It was easier to pretend that these hurtful experiences never happened, or so I thought. After being rejected and abandoned by Sam, the young man I loved, I pursued long hours at work. Numerous college classes and relationships filled the crushing void in my heart. The painful memories of the abortion were swallowed up in perpetual busyness.

Many children who have suffered from sexual abuse turn to drugs, alcohol, and illicit sexual activity. That was not the case for me. In my efforts to block these shameful memories, which now included an abortion, I became a driven over-achiever, always pushing myself harder to get through college, as I worked full-time to provide for my tuition. I was exhausted. I often felt like I was running alongside myself. It was debilitating trying to keep up with all the activities and goals I had set to distract myself from the pain. For me, keeping busy was socially acceptable and culturally honorable.

Although I did not grow up in a religious family, there was moral confusion that flickered within me regarding the abortion. My thoughts of God were of a detached, austere holy man with crossed arms looking down at me with a scowl on his face. He must have been terribly angry and disgusted with the choices I had made. Surely, I would not be welcome near His throne room. Why would He consider ever wanting a relationship with me? Why would He want to even look at me after the decisions I had made? If there was a God, what was this God like?

My father came from a Catholic background and served as an altar boy in the Church. He attended mass like an honorable young Hispanic boy. He took communion and wore the white robe like the priest at his Parrish. My mother, on the other hand, was a Methodist. She didn't care for the Catholic rituals and the drama that went along with it. They didn't agree on religion or discuss the importance of raising us within the structure of a godly foundation. My exposure to church was usually by attending a wedding or a funeral.

When we were very young, my sisters and I were infrequently taken to a Baptist church by a family friend. This stopped the day some elders came over asking for tithes. Despite my lack of understanding about the accessibility to a loving God who would embrace me with forgiveness, I knew morally that something was wrong. What happened to me the day I gave up my child created a wall of shame that would keep me from wanting to be around any church.

2

THE INVISIBLE HAND OF PROTECTION

With time you can learn where to go for nourishment,
where to hide for protection, where to turn for
guidance. Just as your earthly house is a place of
refuge, so God's house is a place of peace.

—Max Lucado[1]

During my first year of college, a classmate of mine saw that I had invested in some additional books to do a sociology report. He and I became friends and I enjoyed sharing with him what we were learning in class. We went out for coffee a few times. On one occasion, he asked me if he could borrow some of my personal books to complete a report that was required for our class. A few weeks after our assignments had been completed, I asked for my books back. He told me he would only give them to me if I would go to his apartment to pick them up—alone. This didn't settle well with me. I felt betrayed, and that he had fooled me into loaning him my books.

Although I was not a believer at the time, I felt the Lord guiding and protecting me. There was something very dark about this young man. I didn't trust his motives. Warily, I decided to cut my losses and not reclaim the books I loaned him. I was not willing to go to his apartment, alone, to get them.

During that same college year, I had a wonderful friend named Mohammad. His family was from Iran, and he was here attending college on a short-term visa. He had another family member who lived in the area; a cousin who owned a restaurant close to the college. He took me there to eat and meet his cousin.

Mohammed and I attended several classes together. I felt I could trust him as a friend. We had much in common: close family relationships, strong work ethic, cultural traditions that framed our lives, and a desire for a good education. We often hung out after class. When the semester ended, he asked me again to go have lunch at his cousin's restaurant. There he presented a very intriguing proposal.

Carefully, he asked me if I would consider marrying him so he could gain his U.S. citizenship. He told me that he and his family had been discussing this option. They wanted me to travel to London alone, and they were willing to pay me $100,000. After arriving in London, they would pay for another ticket to fly me to Iran where I would meet him and his family. There we would have a traditional wedding ceremony. They would offer me another $100,000 after we had been married 6 months. We would, however, need to live together in Iran for up to a year before we could return to the United States. After that, we could live apart in the United States, but to avoid an appearance of fraud under American immigration laws, we would maintain our marital status for three years before divorcing. There would be a bonus of another $100,000 when our divorce was final.

Mohammad knew I didn't love him. He didn't love me. This was not a romantic arrangement, but it was important to him to gain his citizenship so he could fulfill the things he wanted to do in America. Due to the long list of immigrants awaiting access into the United States from the Middle East, he and his family believed this was the best and fastest way for him to remain in the U.S. as a legal immigrant. He had plans to open a business with his cousin and wanted to avoid the legal paperwork.

At the time, I must admit, this was a rather enticing offer. I was working several jobs to pay for my tuition and books. It was an uphill climb financially to continue with my education as well as the car repairs I was experiencing. With my learning disability, it took me longer than the average student to complete my classes. I could only take a few courses at a time to ensure I was able to process the information accurately. Mohammed's offer would eliminate my need to work so hard to complete my education. I could finally afford to hire tutors to help me with the various classes in which I struggled. I could also move out of my parents' house into an apartment and pay off my car—or even purchase a more reliable one. There were so many possibilities that could free me from the stress of my current life. The pressure of getting my education on a limited budget and extended timeframe was daunting to say the least.

However, getting married to someone I didn't love and giving this honor away for financial purposes was sadly disappointing to me. One of the conditions from Mohammed was that I could not share this proposal with anyone—especially my family. I'm sure he did not want anyone to convince me that this was an inappropriate request, not to mention illegal and unsafe. He didn't know the heartache I carried. It was crucial for me to choose wisely in my relationships. I was still hurting from the loss of my boyfriend, Sam. I would not sell my hope of marriage for money.

The dream of marrying someone who really loved me was the true desire of my heart. My hope was to stand before God when I gave my heart in marriage because I was ready to love, honor, and respect my husband all the days of my life—not because someone waved a golden carrot in front of me and seduced me with cash for their own gain, specifically in this case, their permanent immigration status. The temptation to alleviate the stress and struggle of financial pressure would have been a huge bonus. Yet, I firmly decided to decline the offer. I wanted to wait and raise a family together with someone who truly loved me and who would joyfully share in the gift of God's blessings.

I told Mohammad I would not be able to accept his offer and I hoped we could still be friends. He was greatly disappointed, and our friendship began to weaken. This change caused me to question my trust in what had been a simple, uncomplicated friendship with a classmate. Eventually, I saw him making friends with other American girls. I knew it would only be a matter of time before he presented a similar offer to them as well.

During the months and years that followed, political upheaval grew in Iran. This volatile country had its leader of nearly 40 years overthrown. The Shah, Mohammad Reza Shah Pahlavi, had maintained a pro-Western Foreign Policy and fostered economic development in Iran. Military coups disrupted normal peaceful living and thus began the Iranian Revolution. This would usher in the Iranian Shiite cleric, Ayatollah Khomeini, who lead the revolution that overthrew the Shah in 1979.[2] In retrospect, I see the hand of God protecting me from a potentially dangerous and untenable situation.

After graduating from college, my sisters and I decided to have a fun weekend in San Francisco. We flew to the Bay Area from our different locations in California. We had great plans of sightseeing, catching up on our lives, and taking a break from the stresses of life. All three of us were looking for ways of achieving peace, both internally and in our external worlds. The news media was flooded with reports of riots and killings on college campuses. This was a time of great civil unrest across universities in America along with heated opinions regarding the Vietnam War.

It was a beautiful afternoon strolling along Fisherman's Wharf as we looked at handmade jewelry and pottery created by vendors. A nice looking young man with an inviting smile approached us. He began talking to us about our visit to San Francisco. The conversation quickly moved to the state of turmoil in society. He desired peace in our country; we were interested and engaged in the conversation. Some of his friends were getting together to talk about ways we could find peace. They were having a vegetarian dinner to welcome like-minded people. It seemed like a good idea to us as he was not pushy with his rather innocent and caring approach. Since this was a subject we had been talking about, it seemed like a great opportunity. We wanted to talk to other people about how we could live peacefully together.

Later that afternoon, we took a taxi to the address he gave us. Located in an upscale part of town, it was a beautiful, old Victorian home complete with ornate molding. Situated on a corner lot with a well-manicured front yard and a welcoming dark oak entryway, this was an impressive home. Inside, there were about ten people seated around a long table with delicious, healthy vegetarian food talking casually. The host made introductions, and we engaged in small talk for a while. Generous portions of food were flowing from the kitchen. After eating a scrumptious meal and getting to know one another, we were invited to step into a side room where a television monitor was set up to show us a convincing film about our current societal issues. The violence of our society was unmistakable. Discouragement filled the room after watching the hatred and civil unrest displayed in the film.

Following this film, a stocky, middle-aged woman entered the room. She embellished on all the horrible events we had just witnessed. Then she smoothly segued into a convincing solution of a communal farm where people could live together, grow healthy food, and help each other. We would live together like a loving family. This friendly environment was outside the conflict, stress, and turmoil of our daily problems and away from the city. As a matter of fact, the delicious food we had eaten for dinner had been grown at a farm such as this. Excitement ran high in the room. Several people were interested in going to see this utopian, cultural paradise.

Conveniently, they had a van ready that night to take us to see just how great it was. My sisters and I huddled and talked quietly together. We were feeling like our weekend of reconnecting as sisters had begun to derail. Quickly, we decided to recalibrate and focus on the purpose of our trip, which was to spend time together—just the three of us. The organizers of this presentation were not pleased with our decision, but we told them we had already paid for our airline tickets to return home and didn't have extra time to spend at their ranch. The leader's quick change of demeanor was noteworthy. My sister, Lynn, emphasized that she had a husband and children expecting her to return home at a specific time. This seemed to quench the fervency of getting us to go to the farm with them and the other willing participants that night. Many of the other attendees were single and without family responsibilities—or the likelihood of someone reporting their absence. Little did the others know what was ahead for them.

We promptly thanked the organizers for the dinner and told them we needed to return to our hotel as we were expecting calls from our families. While the stocky woman was preoccupied talking to the new, enthusiastic recruits, we were able to exit quickly with our male friend giving us a ride back to our hotel. The following day we saw a play together, and we continued with our plans for the sisters-weekend without an awareness of the spiritual warfare that had been fought to keep us from going to *the farm.*

Fast forward several months: my sister, Lynn, was sitting in a hair salon reading a People magazine. She came across an article about a cult that seduced young people by inviting them to an innocent, vegetarian dinner. They showed a film about the decline of our society and then convinced them to visit their communal farm. She saw a picture of the woman who had addressed our group with her dogmatic rhetoric about escaping our daily lives in the city and joining their *family-friendly* farm. In the article, this same woman was accused of verbally abusing and beating people who had visited the farm but wanted to leave. Those people never returned to their homes. They joined the farm, faithfully seeking harmony, love, family acceptance, and security. Tragically, they received none of that. Many of these naïve, young people were brainwashed. Some didn't see their family and friends for years.

The cult was reported to the police by parents of missing young adults. They were charged with deceptively luring unsuspecting altruists and brainwashing them to remain in the cult. Often, they would convince them to donate their money and possessions for the good of the cult as well as relinquish all family ties. Several parents hired private investigators to find their children and bring them back to their families. Not all of them were successful. You can imagine the overwhelming relief of my sisters and me that we didn't go with them in the van that night. Once again, God's hand was on me and my sisters protecting us from the unthinkable.

"Though I walk in the midst of trouble, you preserve my life; you stretch out your hand against the wrath of mine enemies, and your right hand delivers me" (Psalms 138:7, ESV).

3

THE UGLY HEAD OF MY LEARNING DISABILITY ERUPTS

I, myself, was always recognized . . . as the "slow one" in the family. It was quite true, and I knew it and accepted it. Writing and spelling were always terribly difficult for me. My letters were without originality. I was . . . an extraordinarily bad speller and have remained so until this day.

—Agatha Christie[1]

After graduation from high school, I worked at the Metropolitan Water District of Southern California. I was hired to work in the purchasing department typing up important bids for water management. Every day I went in early and I stayed late to proofread my typing. Fortunately, I was a good typist, averaging 80 words per minute with few errors—until I had to type numbers. Most of my numbers came out reversed even though I repeated them several times in my head. My coworker and I would proofread our work every day. She always made big red circles around my incorrect numbers. I hated seeing all those red circles.

Roland was the head of the purchasing department. He was a kind man of short stature and had a calming voice. I knew he admired my determination as he watched me come in early and stay late each day then run off to classes after work trying to complete my college degree. One day, he called me into his office. Looking rather somber, he asked me to sit down. With controlled speech, he told me they had just awarded a bid to the wrong company, because I had transposed the bid amount. It was a $50,000 error! He knew my aspirations were not to remain as a typing clerk. Roland encouraged me to go back to school and finish my degree. Grateful for his honesty, I handed in my resignation. Within a few days, I had signed up for more classes at The University of California at Los Angeles (UCLA).

Due to my reading challenges, I took fewer classes, and it took me a few years longer to graduate from college. I was finally able to complete all my requirements, receiving a degree in Liberal Arts from UCLA. This was a tremendous accomplishment for me. I was one of the first in my immediate and extended family to complete a college degree. My family was proud of me; I was proud of myself. Life was looking promising again.

My first job after graduation was at the Los Angeles Shelter for Battered Women. It seemed fitting. I was drawn to this job so I could wrap myself around other people's hurt and ignore my own. Witnessing the cyclical abuse in families was a true heartbreak. I worked tirelessly, picking up children from school and taking them to the shelter to live with their sequestered mothers and siblings. Receiving donations of clothes and food, which helped keep the shelter running, occupied much of my day. Overwhelmed with the need for legal representation for these throwaway families, I felt led to search for avenues that could provide a door of hope for their shattered lives.

On several occasions, I hand-walked a battered woman through the court maze of paperwork. My objective was to walk out with a temporary restraining order to protect her and her children from their abuser. This effort often took up my entire work day. I was falling further behind in other job responsibilities. It was impossible to address the needs of so many women at the shelter. So I started a program to help low-income women obtain temporary restraining orders from the abusive men in their lives. I called numerous attorneys to establish a pro bono panel to provide free legal assistance for these marginal women. My passion to rescue others led me to apply to law school on a quest to provide legal representation for those abused, abandoned, and neglected by society.

Although my Law School Admission Test (LSAT) scores were very low, I had some glowing letters of recommendation from my professors from high school, college, and people I had worked with in community service. All of this, combined with my zealous persistence to obtain a legal education, finally resulted in being accepted to a private law school. This was such an exciting and hopeful time for me. My parents were filled with pride that they, who were not able to finish high school themselves, now had a daughter who was going to be an attorney. This was my chance to redeem myself from the mistakes I had made and the shame I carried inside.

However, completing my undergraduate credits by going part-time—this had allowed me enough time to read all the required material—would soon prove I was not prepared for the intense law school curriculum. I was not aware of the rigors of this demanding program. It was tremendously difficult on my health, self-esteem, and relationships.

While attending law school full-time, my undiagnosed learning disability began to surface. I was exhausted all the time from staying up late to finish reading long detailed cases. It was taking its toll on my health. I was losing weight, and my hair began to fall out. Despite my weakened state, I drug myself to class each day. Hearing how other students finished their homework before midnight was always troubling. How was it that they could finish so quickly and understand what they were reading? I needed to read out-loud to myself to hear the words audibly. I used several colored markers to identify different parts of each case. In addition, I always had a legal pad at my side to outline the case in front of me so I could summarize the main points. Then I had to review each case before class so I could remember it. This was an arduous task. It was necessary for me in order to understand each individual case I read. Given there were an average of five cases to read per class and I was enrolled in six classes, the sum of thirty cases a night was monumental.

Towards the end of my first year of law school before final exams, I was hospitalized with an intestinal disorder caused by stress. Having pushed myself for months to stay current with my coursework, I was now doubled over in pain and needed to withdraw from school to recover. My body had been pushed to its limit, and I was no longer able to digest my food. The doctors feared I had a blockage. They wanted to operate and do exploratory surgery. Thankfully, my mother stepped in firmly telling the doctors this was not necessary. I just needed rest. I was checked out of the hospital and brought back to my parents' house to recover. After getting back on my feet, I re-enrolled and attempted my first year again. I couldn't see how punishing this was to my mind and body. Additionally, this required another set of student loans for tuition, books, and housing.

It would be during final exams of that second go-around that I would be excluded from continuing the pursuit of my Juris Doctorate degree. I was unable to finish my exams because I couldn't finish reading the exam packet in time. Several of my professors asked me to meet with them to discuss what happened on the tests. I told them I didn't finish reading the exam. The look on their faces was startling. They asked me if I had ever been tested for a learning disability. They questioned how this could happen when I was able to recite my cases in their classrooms using the rigorous Socratic Method yet not be able to finish reading the exam packet within the timed period. This was the first time I had been told there could be a reason why I had so much difficulty reading and comprehending information.

Unknown to these professors were some warning signs of Dyslexia: a large discrepancy between verbal skills and reading ability; poor written composition; needing to read a page two or three times to understand it; confusing the letters "b" and "d" or "p" and "q," especially when under stress or fatigue. Frequently, Dyslexics perform poorly on standardized tests.[2] Fortunately, I had always scored high enough verbally to get around doing a written report. I could stand up and give an oral report to receive a passing grade and had relied on this strategy. But in a strictly timed exam setting, there was no way around it. Accommodations for learning disabilities were not available at the time I was attending law school, so continuing was out of the question.

All the teachers throughout my schooling were unfamiliar with the symptoms of a learning disability. Frustrated and afraid that it made them look bad on state standardized tests, they often showed little patience with me and others like me who remained undiagnosed. Several times, teachers made comments on my report cards like:

"She doesn't try hard enough."

"She's lazy when it comes to reading."

"She gives good oral reports because she doesn't want to write a report."

"She doesn't try hard enough, so she doesn't do well on timed tests."

These inaccurate statements would follow me throughout school. It was burned in my own psyche; I just needed to try harder to be accepted.

After leaving the halls of legal education, paying back student loans would be my goal for the next fifteen years. It was important for me to honor the debts I incurred, even though I was not able to achieve the degree I desired. I wanted to be sure another label, *defaulting on student loans*, was not added to my list of negative self-talk. I pressed on with fervor, striving to become someone accepted and respected for my skills and unique talents.

Years later while researching ways to help my youngest son I would find out that I struggled with Dyslexia, a learning difference that affected my ability to read and comprehend quickly. This prevented me from completing my law school exams within the designated time-frame. Research shows that this condition is highly hereditary. My father struggled with reading and comprehension all his life. He didn't pick up a book to read until he was in his late 70's. He never knew what it was that made reading so difficult for him. Unfortunately, he was unable to finish high school due to this learning challenge. During the 1940's, young men were encouraged to leave school to help support their families during World War II, so this made it easier for him to exit school and join the workforce.

Not being able to complete my law degree was another disappointment. There was frustration with myself, coupled now with financial pressure to pay back student loans. The search for another career option to support myself took up all my energy. Law school was another dream, one I hoped would bring me respect and fulfillment. It was taken away, and I struggled to understand why.

4

A LIFE-CHANGING DECISION

Come to me all you who are weary and burdened,
and I will provide rest. Take my yoke upon you
and learn from me, for I am gentle and humble
in heart and you will find rest for your souls.

—Matthew 11:28-29

few years later, Lynn invited me to a Christian Women's Luncheon. I had seen some positive changes in her life, and marriage, after she became a believer. At the time, I was unemployed and in an unstable relationship. I had been living with my boyfriend and wanted to get married, but he wasn't ready to make that commitment. Discouraged and hopeless, I told myself, "What could it hurt to spend some time with my sister, even if it was at a luncheon for *straight-laced* women."

It was there I heard the gospel message of Jesus Christ from a professional woman I respected. She was a surgical nurse who had put herself through college after her husband abandoned her and her two daughters. Her story resonated deep within me, and I was drawn to what she had to say. Every word she uttered seemed to be especially for me. There was a peace and confidence in her that I wanted. It wasn't based on pride or self-sufficiency. This was different. I couldn't explain it she had a calm determined presence unlike anything I had ever seen. She spoke freely about God's great love for me and His amazing forgiveness of my sins. My emotions ran down my face as I accepted Jesus Christ as my Lord and Savior. I desperately wanted the peace and forgiveness He offered. Unfortunately, as a new believer I wouldn't be discipled in my new-found faith until several years later, and I continued to flounder.

"He brought me out of a horrible pit (of tumult and destruction), out of the miry clay, and set my feet upon a rock, steadying my footsteps and establishing my path" (Psalm 40:2-3, Amplified Bible).

Going back to the apartment, I shared with my boyfriend I was different now. I knew with everything in me that our living arrangement was wrong. It felt like a mistake. Even though I still cared for him and wanted to marry him, I could no longer live with him without being married. I went up to our bedroom alone. I opened the French doors that looked out over a row of trees down our street and sat on the bed. There I bowed my head and asked God for clear direction. I quietly said, "Please show me a sign, Lord, if you want me to leave this relationship." When I looked up, a beautiful white butterfly flew gently into our bedroom and danced around for what seemed like a few minutes. I was in disbelief. I had never seen this before. It was my sign. The next day I began looking for another place to live.

During the next several months, I sought affirmation from work and relationships. I maintained a long-distance relationship with a man I had met as a student in college, and we married in 1984. Dennis was a successful commodity broker and worked long hours—from early morning until late afternoon. He also was a high functioning drug addict, and I thought I could fix him. He was addicted to marijuana and cocaine. I was addicted to fixing him.

In his trade, brokers would offer each other a small vile of cocaine as a *thank you* for acquiring some exotic product. He said cocaine helped him maintain the crazy hours required for his job. His erratic behavior was a daily distraction from the inner turmoil I continued to wrestle with. As a classic codependent, I paid all his debts, carried him emotionally, and tried to clean him up spiritually as well. My life was out of control.

Although Dennis made a profession of faith to the Lord prior to our marriage, his actions afterwards were quite the contrary. Most Sundays I attended church by myself. My heart ached for my husband to join me in pursuing the values he knew were vital to me and critical for a successful marriage.

My biological clock was ticking. I was 33 years old. I desired to have a child and start our family together as we had planned. On most Sundays at church, I would end up sitting behind a lovely family with a beautiful baby. Holding back the tears, I wondered if I would ever have what I longed for. At every church event I attended, there were children everywhere. These precious little ones reminded me of my maternal ache. Everyone I knew that was my age or younger had already started a family. My longing for a child was ever present. But amidst the turbulent white-water rapids of our marriage, I didn't know how it would work. Despite my current longing for a child and having been able to conceive years earlier, I didn't understand why I couldn't conceive now; we never used contraceptives. Looking back, I had to believe this was God's hand of protection. He knew what was coming.

It didn't make any sense to me that Dennis had promised he would work for the things we agreed upon before marriage—children and a family together—but now had no interest in making them happen. Instead he put more effort into his job, friends, and getting his next high. I attended counseling alone at my church for several months.

My counselor told me the marriage could not heal, and we could not move forward together unless Dennis joined me in discussing our marital issues. After several months of asking him to come with me if he wanted our marriage to succeed, he came along. Reluctantly, he sat in the counseling office with his arms crossed. He responded to the counselor's questions like he was engaged in a quick tennis match. He slammed back his answers before the counselor could get them out of her mouth. If body language was any indication of his true intent in working toward salvaging our marriage, then it was game over.

Again, I pushed hard with my career at a Fortune 500 company, searching for my identity and something to satisfy the heartache. My despair began to surface, and I was soon falling apart at my job. With support from a compassionate employer, I checked myself into a 30-day hospital program for codependency. I began a slow journey of unraveling years of painful secrets. After a turbulent three-and-a-half-year marriage, and two separations, we divorced. Dennis told me he didn't want any of this *God stuff* in his life and decided he didn't want to be married any longer. The residue of unfulfilled dreams and a large IRS debt from Dennis made my life a monumental task. My issues of insecurity and self-worth were at an all-time low. I was divorced, childless, and 33 years-old. Additionally, I was a blight to my parents—a cultural misfit within my Latino culture.

For months after our separation and divorce, I received phone calls and sometimes visits from Dennis' friends. They sought me out regarding money he had borrowed during our short marriage. They felt betrayed and angry that he was unavailable to pay back his *loans*. He didn't return their phone calls and even changed jobs. Initially, I tried to pay back what I could afford. But eventually, through the help of my counselor, I was able to direct them to him. I would not take ownership of his wrong decisions. His choices were not a reflection of my character, and it took me a while to understand that.

Over a year later, while attending Al-Anon meetings for my co-dependency issues, I met a friendly, enthusiastic, fast-talking, quick-witted man who was kind and attentive to me. After several requests to go out with him, I decided to go out for a cup of yogurt. I wanted to take it slow. We walked on the beach, talking and laughing. I was laughing so hard I nearly dropped my yogurt. He was quick with jokes and full of life. Life was beginning to come back into focus for me. It was a pleasant change from my previous marriage to a narcissistic, out-of-control drug user.

Being around Oscar was like a fun ride at a carnival. He was entertaining, full of stories, and extremely funny. My sides hurt from laughing so much after spending time with him. His quick wit, keen mind, and memory for detailed facts always amazed me. He was generous and thought of ways to make me feel important and cherished. He lavished me with gifts, cards, and expensive dinners on a regular basis. Time spent with him was never dull.

Oscar told me he was a former undercover officer for the Los Angeles Police Department (LAPD). It had been his dream since he was a little boy. However, given his mechanical abilities, he had gone into the automotive industry directly from high school. He was a quick learner and technically savvy. Oscar excelled in the automotive industry. After doing some soul-searching about his true passion, he took a few years off to fulfill his dream of becoming a police officer. He desired to make a contribution to society and believed this was the best-suited career for him.

While in the Police Academy he was pulled out to do undercover work because he could pass for a young drug dealer. He worked several dangerous assignments. However, when he wanted to transfer from being undercover to another department, he was told he couldn't because he was so good at what he did. So Oscar decided to quit the police department and he went back to the car industry. That is when I met him; he was a service manager for a high-end dealership.

Oscar swept me off my feet with beautiful jewelry, romantic picnics, concerts, and stories of his near-death experiences while working undercover for LAPD. Being around him made me feel safe, and his knowledge of police work made me feel protected. It was the first time in my life I felt like someone was looking out for me. There was a strong sense of security just being around him and his knowledge of the law.

On one of our first dates he told me the tragic story of his brother, Glen. An Air Force pilot, Glen had been shot down while serving our country during Desert Storm. Oscar told me not to mention this when I met his parents as they were still emotionally distraught from the loss of their son. Of course, I honored his request and never mentioned his brother's name. Pictures of Glen in uniform were sprinkled throughout Oscar's parents' home, and I felt sad for their tremendous loss.

After a whirlwind year of dating, Oscar proposed to me in front of my family on Christmas Eve. The wedding date was set. His fervent determination to make me his bride continued until our wedding day. We attended Christian marriage counseling with our church pastor. Excitedly, we planned a European honeymoon together. There, while sightseeing castles and beautiful countryside, we were able to stay with his family at least for a portion of our time. Life was back in full color. My heart was dancing with joy.

Oscar had charmed me with his humor and convinced me he wanted a Christian marriage and family. My friends and family liked him and were fascinated by his stories of undercover police work. Things were finally changing for me and I felt protected. Life was taking a positive turn, and I was ready to stop the crazy cycle of running from my internal script.

Finally, I felt secure. We married and had two wonderful sons: Isaac and Nathan.

One Christmas Day, early in our marriage, we visited Oscar's parents. Everyone was enjoying a splendid day of my mother-in-law's fabulous food and extravagant desserts. After opening our presents, there was a knock on the door. We were excited that someone had stopped by with his wife to celebrate with the family. He looked familiar, but I didn't know who it was. You can imagine the shock I experienced when I was told it was Glen, Oscar's deceased brother! He walked right into my in-laws' home during the Christmas celebration. Oscar quickly whispered to me Glen had been missing in action, and it was a top-secret mission that could not be discussed. Still new to the family, I didn't ask any questions and respected their privacy about the matter. Later, I would find out this had been fabricated to enlist my sympathy as part of a greater plan.

Almost a year into our marriage, I became pregnant. We were living in a cute apartment by the beach and were growing out of our small place. Oscar and I had discussed purchasing a home before we married and now was the time to move on it. Before we welcomed the birth of our son, Isaac, we went shopping for a home. After being blessed with two baby showers, there was hardly any room to move around in our small one-bedroom place. We drove around for months in the heat of summer with our realtor trying to find a house that fit our budget. Finally, as my swollen feet could barely walk through another potential home, we found a reasonable starter home and placed a bid on it. Our bid was accepted, and the paperwork began to roll.

Oscar had worked in the automotive field before and after his time in the police force. Prior to our marriage, he told me he had invested over twenty-five thousand dollars in his 401k account. He wanted to use it for a down payment on our first home.

When the time came to disclose our financial resources, Oscar stated he was having trouble reaching the people who could help him retrieve his money from Toyota. He was frustrated trying to call them from work during his breaks and lunch hour. He said he couldn't get a hold of anyone after work because they were in a different time zone. Given the sense of urgency, he decided to talk to his parents about borrowing the money from them upfront. He would pay them back when his 401k money was released.

This sounded like a reasonable request. Oscar's parents were willing to loan us the money from their savings so we could make the down-payment on our first home. They withdrew the money from their retirement savings account, and we received a cashier's check from them. We were then able to sign all our loan documents. Everything was moving in the right direction. We would now be in a bigger place and could set up the nursery and baby items for our soon arriving son.

Shortly after we moved into our new place, Isaac was born. The elated grandparents came to the hospital to see their precious new grandson, and it was a joyful time. My heart was filled with gratitude to the Lord for this precious gift of life. I was also deeply grateful to my new in-laws for their willingness to loan us the money to get into our much-needed home. Without them and their desire to help us, we would still be in a cramped apartment.

A few months later, my in-laws began calling to find out about the money Oscar had in his 401k. At first, he told them that the office had moved to another state and he wasn't able to get ahold of anyone. Then he said that they were in a different time zone, and he was unable to call while anyone was there. It was one excuse after another. After several weeks of going back and forth with escalating phone calls between Oscar and his parents, he stopped answering their calls. Then one day, he inadvertently answered the phone to hear his father's voice.

A huge argument ensued which lead to them not speaking to us for over a year.

This was devastating to me. I was horrified with the way Oscar had flippantly disregarded his promise to pay back his parents. Family relationships were very important to me and honoring our debt was a way of showing respect to others. Oscar and I had several heated discussions about getting his money and how he treated his parents. As a nursing, hormonal mother, this was an emotional roller coaster for me. Our conversations always ended up with him yelling and throwing something. He then turned around and walked out of the room.

Tearfully, when he was away at work one day, I called my new in-laws to tell them how sorry I was about this terrible situation. They were understandably angry and wondered if I had been part of Oscar's scheme. I told them I believed Oscar had the money but didn't know how to access it. Until that happened, I was willing to take the money out of my own 401k and pay them back with my retirement savings. They said, "We appreciate your willingness to give up part of your retirement, but no thanks. This is between us and our son." They were still very angry with Oscar's lack of respect and betrayal.

Shortly after first meeting their grandson, Isaac, the grandparents didn't come around until he was almost 18 months old. This separation was a loss for them and for us. Eventually, they decided they were not going to get their money back from Oscar. They wanted to put it behind them. Seeing their grandson and participating in his life was more important than receiving the money. They creatively drew up a Living Trust that deducted the twenty-five thousand from Oscar's allocation.

Oscar was never able to retrieve his 401K money from Toyota. He never wanted to discuss it if I brought it up. It was a forbidden topic in our marriage. I never found out if the money ever existed in the first place.

During our fourth year of marriage, Oscar was working for a Lexus dealership as a service manager. They were having an important contest on customer satisfaction surveys. The company was sending the managers with the best ratings from various regions around the country and their wives to Hawaii. This became the topic of conversation every night as Oscar was consumed with winning this contest and going to Hawaii. He spoke excitedly about the awards dinner they were planning at a posh hotel in Kauai. I could see the sparkle in his eyes as he went on and on about how important this award was to him.

At the managers' monthly meetings the Award Banquet in Kauai was a big agenda topic. Also discussed was the beautiful trophy that would be presented to the manager with the top ratings. As the deadline for the contest grew closer, Oscar became ramped up with excitement. His ratings had gone up since the contest began, and this encouraged him. He talked about the other managers and how he felt he could outdo their ranking. Surprisingly, around the time that the results were to come out, Oscar stopped talking about it altogether.

I was careful not to mention the contest, believing he didn't qualify. Since he flew off the handle when things didn't go his way, I didn't want to invite this behavior around our home if it could be helped. It was a tender topic, and I was willing to wait for him to bring it up again.

Soon afterwards, he came home with two round-trip tickets to Hawaii and told me that he had won the trip. We were both excited, but I was surprised in the way he presented this to me. Why did he wait so long to tell me he won the contest after such a long silence? Still I wanted to see him accept an award he had worked hard for and get the recognition he deserved. Additionally, I was looking forward to meeting Oscar's coworkers and to talk with their wives.

Since Oscar didn't keep in touch with any of his coworkers from the police department this was a chance for me to meet some of the people from his current job. We had only attended company events from my job and socialized with some of my coworkers. This was a way for him to connect with the type of work I did and put a face with a name when we shared about our jobs. I wanted the same experience with the job and people Oscar connected with on a daily basis.

My parents agreed to stay at our home and take care of Isaac for that week so we could celebrate Oscar's big accomplishment in Hawaii. We were off on a grand adventure to the Hawaiian Island of Oahu. I asked Oscar why we were going to Oahu when the recognition dinner was in Kauai. He told me that he decided he didn't want to go to the event with everyone else since he saw them every day. That seemed strange to me, and I was disappointed he chose to not be a part of something special like this. Also I felt cheated that I wouldn't be able to meet anyone he worked with, or their wives. But I accepted his decision since he had worked earnestly for this trip, and I was grateful we could take such a beautiful trip together.

Oscar never brought the coveted trophy home from the dealership. He told me that he wanted to leave it at his job, so he could look at it every day and remind others of how hard he had worked for it.

When Isaac was around three years old, I became pregnant with our second child. The thought of another child breathed hope into our sluggish marriage. I had just completed my first trimester, and we had announced the joy of this second child to both our families, our church family, and my friends at work. Plans for the nursery theme and rearranging Isaac's room filled my heart and occupied most of our conversations. Our families and friends were excitedly anticipating this new life with us.

Our small son, Isaac, was ecstatic with excitement that he was going to be a big brother. He talked about the baby every day. He wanted to know what the baby would look like, what it would say when it talked to him, and if he could play with it soon? Would the baby sleep in his room so he could keep an eye on it? Would he have to share his toys? So many questions from this tender-hearted boy.

On a normal Sunday morning, while getting ready for church, I began to bleed. Confused and frightened, I screamed to Oscar from the bathroom. We quickly changed plans, dropped off our son at my sister's house, and frantically drove to the hospital. My stomach was cramping, and I was trying to breathe. Everything was happening so fast. I just wanted to push the clock back and feel like a normal pregnant woman. Oscar parked crookedly in the Emergency Room designated parking area and quickly helped me out of the car. Tears were already falling from my eyes.

Immediately, I was wheeled in to have an ultrasound. There I would hear the most horrifying news, and it would shatter my heart. The young doctor on duty clinically said to another resident in training, "I see several detached pieces of the fetus and we will need to perform a Dilation and Curettage (D&C) procedure to remove all additional tissue from her uterus to prevent infection." It was like I wasn't even in the room. I wanted to scream, "That is my baby you're talking about!" My hope and my dreams were dissolving by the minute. Inside my body, screams echoed through the canyons of my heart. My baby had not formed properly, and the body was not intact.

Horrified, my head was spinning and my heart pounding. Tears slid down the side of my face and pooled on the hospital sheets. How could this be? We had so much hope for this baby. Hot tears now covered my face as I tried to gain control of myself. I could barely breathe. Oscar was quiet and detached. He didn't seem to know how to offer comfort in this crisis.

For weeks afterwards, I would cry while making dinner or folding clothes. Oscar would tell me he was going to visit the neighbor and would take Isaac with him to give me some time.

He was so disconnected with his feelings that he couldn't offer me any emotional support. One time when he left the house to *give me some time* my neighbor, Kerry, came over with some flowers and a tray of food for my dinner. She told me she had lost a baby and remembered how hard it was to move on. She also noticed that Oscar was spending a lot more time at her house these days. Despite my husband's inability or desire to console my aching heart, God had sent a friend who reached out to me in my pain. This was a tender time of friendship between two women who had both lost a precious baby.

"For He has not despised or scorned the suffering of the afflicted one; he has not hidden his face from him but has listened to his cry for help" (Psalm 22:24).

Memories of the abortion surfaced after my miscarriage, and I wondered if I was being punished for having had an abortion nearly twenty-years earlier. Depression and sorrow were unwanted companions to my daily routine. It was hard to shake the feeling of low self-worth from my past *choice*. I pressed through my work days, and I pushed back the huge disappointment that I was no longer expecting a beautiful baby to hold, cuddle, love, and raise with our son.

Coming home and telling Isaac that the baby he was excited to meet was now in Heaven was one of my most difficult conversations. His three-year-old mind couldn't understand why his Mommy's tummy still looked like a baby was there. "Where is Heaven?" he asked. "And how do you get there? Can I go see what the baby looks like, Mommy? Why didn't he want to come be with us?" Such heartbreak accompanied his sweet questions. Most of the time, I just prayed with him and asked him to pray when he thought about it for another brother or sister.

Well that was enough to move his little heart in a prayerful direction. He began to pray morning, noon, and night for a little brother. I would remind him that God could bring us a brother or a sister. Only God could decide what He would choose to bless our family with. But no, he was fervent in his decision. He said, "No, Mommy I only want a brother, not a sister, and God is going to give me one." And with just that kind of determination before each meal and at night before he went to bed, Isaac would bow his little head, fold his chubby little fingers, and deliberately pray for a little brother.

Now at the age of 39 my doctor told me we could try again, but the chances for success may be less likely due to my age and having had a miscarriage already. We prayed and continued to hear the sweet prayers of our only son. Within a month I was green with nausea and had a confirmed pregnancy. This was a joyous time of God's faithfulness in allowing me to become pregnant with another child. Once again, my heart began to fill with the hope this new life stirred within me.

During my fifth month of pregnancy I began to bleed and was consumed with fear and anxiety at the thought of losing another baby. Waking up with clenched jaws and massive headaches didn't help my current condition. My doctor examined me and put me on bed rest for the remainder of my pregnancy. Those four months were tearful as I could not pick up our son, Isaac. I needed to remain in bed for what seemed like an eternity. Isaac would stand next to my bed and beg me to play with him. He didn't understand why I had to lay in bed when it wasn't bedtime. The hardest thing for me, was not being able to roll around and rough house with my son. We enjoyed our time together. Now that I had to rest much of the day, it was hard on him and a challenge to my heart. Isaac didn't understand why I could not be his fun, playful, mommy any longer. I needed to protect the son I was carrying: Nathan. Regularly, I reassured Isaac that he was precious to me and deserved the time I could give him.

Again, the hand of God was with us as our friends, family and church came alongside to offer help during this difficult season. They brought food, offered to clean our home, and took

Isaac to the park so he could be a little boy and run around. This was an answer to my prayer before it was even uttered.

During those long months, I journaled, read, and prayed. It was a challenge to keep perspective and obey the doctor's orders. My hopes and prayers were that staying in bed would result in a healthy baby. Thankfully, after that long inactive time, Nathan was born. He was a beautiful cherub who arrived at five in the morning, weighing a healthy 9 pounds, 2 ounces.

Wow! He was gorgeous and one look at him erased the grueling 20 hours of labor, excruciating suction process, and ultimately another cesarean delivery. Watching Isaac greet his baby brother for the first time was a surreal joy. I got to see the consistent, faithful, fervent prayers of a little boy come to life before my eyes. I felt like he knew something clearly in his heart about having a little brother that caused him not to waiver, but to press forward in prayer for what he desired most. What a lesson that would be for me.

Nathan's birth was around the time the movie, *The Lion King*, was released. We had taken Isaac to see it and bought him the movie. He saw it over and over, and we sang the songs together. His heart was set on naming his baby brother *Simba*, because he looked like the cute lion cub in the movie. Isaac wanted to lift him up and offer him to the jungle like he saw in the film. Fortunately, he wasn't the one naming his brother. He could barely lift him while safely sitting on the couch, let alone lift him over his head.

During the boys' early years, we did normal things as a family. We enjoyed our two dogs, had barbeques, took walks around the neighborhood, rode bikes together, attended Isaac's baseball games, and attended church and family events. The boys enjoyed hanging out with their dad, going to the car parts store, or working on their bikes while Oscar worked on the family car. For the most part, life together was pretty normal, with intermittent outburst of anger from Oscar. We had grown used to it, and it seemed normal to us.

His anger seemed to be the result of losing a series of jobs and other deeper issues. I, on the other hand, kept my focus on keeping my corporate job, taking care of the kids, and doing the housework—especially when Oscar was frustrated. Working full-time and carrying the medical insurance so we could have guaranteed coverage was not an option. This was vital since both the boys and I had asthma. We had already spent several nights in the Emergency Room (ER) when the boys caught a cold and had trouble breathing. After frequenting the ER, we were sent home with a nebulizer machine to assist with their respiratory issues. A few hospital stays later, with long nights listening to my sons' struggle to breathe due to bronchial asthma, I was determined to keep my job for the medical benefits my boys needed.

Truly, I wanted to experience being a full-time mom. I didn't want to get suited up for a corporate job every day and leave my boys in daycare. But I couldn't trust Oscar's inconsistent job record. We needed medical insurance and it wasn't a negotiable issue.

Our sons were intrigued by the exciting stories of their father and enjoyed sharing them with their friends. One of the more memorable events was the time he told them he wore a beard because he had been shot in the chin during a bank robbery. Fortunately, his full beard covered his facial scar—a scar that was a reminder of that fateful day. Lucky to be alive, he didn't want a daily reminder of that experience by seeing a large, ugly scar.

Oscar told the boys he had been pulled out of the police academy without finishing because he had a young face. He was needed to participate in a large drug bust at a gang-filled high school. Oscar was used as an undercover officer to gather information from ring leaders about drug warehouses. He portrayed a delinquent student who was heading up a drug ring at the high school. Oscar even had a girlfriend at the school and attended drug parties with her to get the layout of the homes. While inside, he would go into the restroom and draw the floorplan of the house on toilet paper. After taking his girlfriend home he would meet his police contacts and give them the information. Soon afterward those same houses would be surrounded by police officers with search warrants. His stories were riveting with precise details of dates, times, penal codes, and names of the officers with whom he worked.

5

SIGNS OF CHANGE

Fear not, for I am with you; be not dismayed, for I am your God. I will strengthen you, I will help you, I will uphold you with my righteous right hand.

—Isaiah 41:10 ESV

It wasn't long after our honeymoon that I sensed a change of heart from my husband. His fervor in getting me to marry him had lost momentum. All the months of attentive listening and dreaming together about a life of family, friends, and adventures, was fading like a dull old painting. A darker, depressed, and sometimes troubled side of Oscar had emerged from within his depths, and for the next fourteen years I would struggle looking for the man I had married.

This was the life I had waited 34 years to embrace. I wanted to share my faith, hopes, dreams, and a beautiful family with the man who had promised to share my Christian values in our marriage. Oscar had attended church with me every Sunday for almost a year prior to our marriage. He gave his heart to the Lord while on a motorcycle ride with our pastor.

Convincingly, Oscar told me and others that this was the life he longed for: a stable marriage, raising children together, and participating in church alongside family and friends.

I wasn't going to let my hope or my dreams die. It was my goal, whatever it took, to get back the man I loved and who pursued me with a passion. Books on marriage decorated my nightstand. I signed us up for marriage retreats and seminars in an effort to find what had been lost. This was the father of our precious sons, and I wanted them to have the dad they deserved. I was willing to put my energy into making our marriage good for all of us. The problem was, I was the only one trying.

Oscar had a son from a previous marriage. His name was Michael. He was a sweet boy with sandy blonde hair and a freckled nose, and he spoke with a raspy voice. He had a desperate longing for his father's attention and love. Unfortunately, he rarely got it. Michael tried to show me how to fish and catch frogs on one of our picnic dates. Although Oscar appeared to be genuinely interested in Michael's well-being and included him on a few dates before our marriage, this too would change after the wedding ceremony.

Sadly, Michael wasn't a priority for Oscar. Although I had all of Michael's baseball games on our calendar, his father never attended any of them. Oscar was impatient with him and raised his voice during normal conversations on a regular basis. One time, at a fast food restaurant, Oscar went off on Michael, berating him so loudly that the family at the next table got up and left. I comforted Michael, in as much as he would allow me to, but so much damage had been done.

Stopping the rage and volume of anger that quickly spewed out of Oscar's mouth was another of my goals. Somehow, over time, I had grown to see it as normal behavior and made excuses for his inappropriate outbursts. My fear controlled my reactions, and I wanted to protect our sons from further emotional outbursts. All my efforts went into keeping my little family together. I pretended that the problem wasn't as obvious as it was to outsiders looking in. Everybody had problems, I rationalized, and Oscar was just frustrated by some of life's bad breaks. I had no awareness of Oscar's behavior in his past relationships or the problems he faced growing up with an abusive father.

Most memorable was a time Michael had come to visit during his summer break. I had introduced him to a young boy across the street with the hope he could have someone to play with during his lonely visits. After asking his dad to do something with him and hearing his excuses, Michael stopped seeking his father's attention. Michael and his new neighborhood friend had decided to play basketball at another boy's house down the street but didn't tell us. We began looking for him all over the neighborhood, and we were beginning to panic.

Oscar was livid at the inconvenience it caused him. When he found Michael he followed him home and was yelling so loudly I could hear him several houses away. Michael was crying by this time, not only from the emotional trauma but from being kicked from behind by his father while he was walking back to the house. I couldn't see this until they were closer to our driveway. Michael ran into the house sobbing; I saw the footmarks on the back of his pants.

My heart broke for Michael's deep sadness and humiliation. Seeing the look of a desperate, broken, young boy on his face, filled me with helplessness and anxiety. I didn't know what to do about this growing rage inside my husband. I was frozen with fear and hated the way he behaved. At the same time, I wondered where the torrent of anger Oscar had kept bottled up during our courtship and the first years of our marriage came from.

As Michael grew older and became a teenager, his visits with us were less frequent. When we did see him, he came over with green hair shaved in a mohawk and had a frequent twitch in his face. Rebellion, low grades, and anger replaced this boy's once joyful heart. He was withdrawn and looked like he hated the world. He grunted at his father and ignored his sarcasm. Michael and Oscar were like two planets orbiting around each other but never entering the other's gravitational pull.

Not long after that terrible episode with Michael, I began to see more specific signs of unstable behavior in Oscar: habitual lying, extremely controlling behavior, flirtatiousness with other women, a severe problem with anger, and all with a lack of consequences to his behavior. Oscar lost several jobs and relationships due to his anger and rage. We were in and out of counseling for much of our fourteen-year marriage. Unfortunately, I attended most sessions alone.

In 2003, my physical health began to change from all the stress in our turbulent marriage. I developed a large cyst on my neck and was having trouble swallowing. My doctor immediately referred me to a head, nose, and throat surgeon who stuck a large needle in the side of my neck and drained the cyst for sample fluids. Enduring the needle in my neck was a miserable pain that seemed to last far longer than my appointment that afternoon. Fortunately, the cyst was benign, but I was scheduled for surgery within one week.

After three months of recovering from that surgery, I began to bleed for several weeks. I had always had a regular menstrual cycle up until this nonstop bleeding, so I knew something was very wrong. My gynecologist told me I was anemic, had severe endometriosis, and cysts on my ovaries that could turn to cancer. I needed a full hysterectomy as soon as possible.

Oscar was emotionally detached during this time and it made preparing for this extensive surgery all the more difficult. During my hysterectomy Oscar sat with my parents in the waiting room and barely communicated with them. When I was released from post-op and given a regular hospital room, Oscar came in to see me. I was in extreme pain, moaning and moving around the bed in discomfort. The nurse hadn't come in to give me the pain medication yet.

Oscar flipped out in an angry tirade yelling at the nurse down the hall to move her fat ass and get me some pain medication immediately. The look of horror on the face of my parents and the other medical staff was alarming. My body and mind were filled with nausea and confusion. Why was he doing this? If he didn't care about me, then why did he need to yell and act so controlling? The head nurse told him to stop his inappropriate behavior or leave. He stormed out of my room and the hospital.

My parents were terrified for me and begged me to come to their house to recover from surgery. They hadn't witnessed this side of Oscar. And he wasn't hiding it anymore. Willingly, my mom and dad said they would take care of the boys and me until things settled down and I could make some clear decisions. Later, they secretly told me they were frightened that he would not take proper care of me. It could get worse. Our home had several stairs leading up to the second floor and our bedroom. They were concerned about how I would manage going up and down the stairs after surgery—especially with a husband who shifted between indifference and rage.

Oscar returned to the hospital later that night close to the end of visiting hours. He waited until that supervising nurse who had asked him to leave had ended her shift. He slipped in quietly and told me he was angry about the slowness of the nurse and the inadequate medical care I was getting. "It was their fault," he blurted out and he was just being a good husband. I told him that I thought it would be better if I recovered at my parents' house with the boys. This way he could just go to work and he didn't need to take time off to take care of me. He was angry that I was not following his plan. So, once again, he stormed out of the room. The next day, I was released from the hospital, and my parents came to pick me up. I was at their house for nearly a week and hadn't heard anything from Oscar. Finally, I called *him*. He told me I didn't need to come home and should stay at my parents' house longer. His emotional abuse was taking a new turn.

A friend from church told me how uncomfortable she was when she spoke with Oscar because he violated her personal space. This was after she had mentioned it to him several times, and he disregarded it. She was a Human Resource Specialist at a famous museum and had arranged an opportunity for Oscar to work there. He dismissed the warnings and continued to act inappropriately. Eventually, he left that job without making any changes to his behavior. He ended up seeking other employment.

Once while a friend of mine and her son were visiting us, Oscar became extremely angry at our dog, Coco. He picked her up by her chain, nearly choking her in midair, in front of the boys. He threw the dog, who was squealing in pain, into the back of the truck. My son, Nathan, and his friend came running up the stairs frantically telling us what had just happened. I was horrified that Oscar would do this, especially in front of the boys. My girlfriend looked at me and said, "He's not concealing it anymore, Naomi."

She knew of the circumstances of our troubled marriage and could see it from the perspective of an outsider. She told me she didn't feel comfortable being around Oscar and didn't want her son to see any more trauma to our dog. Afraid of what Oscar would do around her children, she and her husband chose not to visit us anymore. That day she cut short the play date and didn't return.

Oscar didn't care how his behavior impacted other people. His signs of rage, emotional abuse, and verbal abuse took their toll on our already broken marriage. One day, he came home from work and told me he was not happy in the marriage. He said he needed a change. However, he was not specific about what he wanted to do. All he did was complain that he wasn't happy. Additionally, told me he was tired of working and driving long hours commuting every day. Although I was not surprised at his discontent with our marriage, the words were hard to hear, especially since he made no effort to make things better. I thought he was having a mid-life crisis—he was in his mid-forties.

Oscar had made friends with a wealthy older woman who sometimes attended our church with her ailing husband. Her husband was several years older than she, and she was overwhelmed taking care of him with his medical issues along with the maintenance of their large ranch. Oscar jumped at the opportunity to be of service, and unbeknownst to me, would stop by after work and offer to help her with chores around the ranch. He invited the woman and her husband over to our house for dinner and worked hard at making a good impression on them.

We, in turn, were invited to visit their lovely home a few times. On one occasion, while her husband was out of the room, she made an inappropriate comment about looking for a younger man when her husband passed away. She said she was lonely and was ready to live again.

Not long after Oscar befriended her, I would hear him whispering on the telephone to this woman about how he wanted to be there for her and lighten her load. When I confronted him with this, he denied having the conversations and told me I was making it up. Soon afterward, Oscar brought home a large recreation vehicle that took up most of our driveway. I questioned why he would make a unilateral decision to purchase something that expensive, and he said it was a gift from a friend. He gave the boys a tour inside and talked about taking some camping trips as a family. I was cautiously hopeful that he was finally making an effort to work on our marriage and invest in our family.

Oscar now agreed to start counseling with a pastor at the church we were attending. I was grateful for his decision to talk with someone. This may begin to turn things around for us and allow him to confront his past hurts. He wasn't consistent with his appointments but seemed to be working on himself and his frustration with life. He still was negative and complained about everyone else that rubbed him wrong. I was hopeful, though, and wanted desperately to make this marriage work.

A few months later, after returning home from a counseling session, Oscar stomped up the stairs, passed me in the kitchen, and marched into our bedroom. I asked him how his session went, but he ignored me. He then walked over to his gun cabinet and pulled out a 9mm gun. Oscar turned to me, racked the slide, and told me he was going to take care of me. He yelled and said he would do likewise to a dear pastor friend of ours that he accused me of having an affair with!

"Keep me safe, O God, for in you I take refuge" (Psalm 16:1).

Oscar blamed me for terrible things and said I had done them to destroy our marriage. He was pacing the floor while waving the gun in the air. This was the craziest I had ever seen him. He was sinking into a greater darkness; it was now life-threatening. Something inside of him had switched, and he became someone I didn't know or understand.

Trembling with fear, and thoroughly confused with this sharp turn, I shot up a frantic prayer to get our youngest son out of the house. I told Oscar I would take Nathan to a friend's house and return quickly so we could talk. While Oscar paced the floor and waved the gun, I quickly grabbed my purse and scooped up our eight-year-old son who was downstairs playing a computer game, unaware of the frightening drama upstairs. I rushed out the door with him.

"No weapon forged against you will prevail, and you will refute every tongue that accuses you" (Isaiah 54:17).

Fortunately, our oldest son, Isaac, was away at a church event for the weekend and didn't experience his father's erratic behavior. It would be difficult for anyone to erase the memory of the insanity of that moment, especially a child. The shock of having my protector change roles and become my adversary seemed like a bad dream; my worst nightmare.

"A quick-tempered man does foolish things" (Proverbs 14:17).

Shaking and fearful, I drove to my friend's house. She had a son Nathan played with. Fortunately, my friend was cleaning her garage with her husband and came out to the driveway to greet us. Seeing the absolute terror on my face, she knew something terrible had happened. Calmly, she directed Nathan to go in the house with her son, and she held me while I cried. She told me I needed to call the police from the safety of her home and not go back to my home until it was safe to do so. It was surreal calling the police on my husband and hearing the words come out of my mouth: "My husband had pulled a gun on me and I've left my home to seek safety with my son." Illogically, my greatest fear was not for my own welfare, but that Oscar would shoot himself or would be sent to jail.

The twisted irony is that the police came to our home, didn't find the hidden gun, heard Oscar's story about being a former Los Angeles undercover police officer, and did not file a report. Oscar told them he had worked for LAPD in their Wilshire Division doing drug busts. Later, this would make things very difficult for me. It would require the arduous task of filing a complaint, waiting several weeks for an appointment, and speaking with a lieutenant to finally get a report filed. Without it, I could not get a restraining order to protect my sons and me.

Oscar denied ever waving a gun at me and said it was just a simple argument. After meeting with our pastor, serious stipulations were made by me to restore our shattered marriage. They included the removal of all weapons from our home, marriage counseling, and anger management counseling. I hung on to the hope that Oscar would want to do whatever it took to restore our battered marriage and keep our family together. He had not made any clear decisions on ending our marriage, and I was hanging on to my prayers that his eyes would be opened to what he could lose.

Oscar worked longer hours and seemed to come home just to go to bed and wake up the next morning to repeat the same pattern. I was busy with our sons' schoolwork, sports and teaching classes for home schooled families. When he was home, tension was high with little, if any, communication between Oscar and me or the boys. He barked out orders and continued to remain in his own bubble of negativity. I decided to take the boys to visit my sister for a week and give Oscar the time he requested to ponder the changes I required to save our marriage. He agreed but never called to check up on us as he usually did when we visited my family. As the week went on, I called our house several times and left messages but never received a return phone call.

It was summertime, and I had taken the boys to get some shorts and shoes. I was surprised that my bank card didn't work when I went to pay for them. My purchase was rejected, and I went to the bank to find out what the problem was. While standing in front of the bank teller she told me I had no money in my account. I asked to speak with a manager and, to my horror, she confirmed the crushing news.

Oscar had transferred the money from our joint savings account into his name exclusively and removed the money from our checking account. This, of course, included the money from my years of working full time when he couldn't hold onto a job. Despite my protest, she told me Oscar was allowed to do this, since he was the one who had set up the accounts and they were under his name and social security number.

"Be strong and courageous. Do not be afraid or terrified because of them, for the Lord your God goes with you; he will never leave you nor forsake you" (Deuteronomy 31:6).

During our time away, Oscar was busy. He had moved the motor home—that he claimed was a gift—to the ranch of his woman friend. At our home, he had placed large, pad-locked chains around the gates leading up to our driveway and boarded all of the windows and doors with large pieces of plywood, drilling screws into the windows to secure the boards. He deliberately told our neighbors that if they saw me to call the police because I had kidnapped our children, and he didn't know if they were dead or alive. Something had snapped inside of my husband, and Oscar now became someone I feared.

Lundy Bancroft[1] in his book, *Why does he do that? Inside the minds of angry and controlling men,* states a rather appropriate observation:

> The woman knows from living with the abusive man that there are no simple answers. Friends say: "He's mean." But she knows many ways in which he has been good to her. Friends say: "He treats you that way because he can get away with it. I would never let someone treat me that way." But she knows that the times when she puts her foot down the most firmly, he responds by becoming his angriest and most intimidating. When she stands up to him, he makes her pay for it—sooner or later. Friends say: "Leave him." But she knows it won't be that easy. He will promise to change. He'll get friends and relatives to feel sorry for him and pressure her to give him another chance. He'll get severely depressed, causing her to worry whether he'll be alright. And, depending on what style of abuser he is, she may know that he will become dangerous when she tries to leave him. She may even be concerned that he will try to take her children away from her, as some abusers do.

6

THE UNVEILING

*Did you ever run for shelter in a storm, and find fruit which
you expected not? Did you never go to God for safeguard,
driven by outward storms, and there find unexpected fruit?*

—John Owen[1]

My sister, Rebecca, invited me to attend a weekend
seminar at her church called, *Recognizing the Signs
of Abuse in Relationships.* I was like many victims
of abuse in that I had taken the unacceptable behaviors for
too long. Now, I was unable to recognize the effects it was
having on me and my sons. It was like the frog who sits in
boiling water and doesn't realize it is getting hotter because
of the slow process; you just get used to it.

Rebecca, her husband, and other family members had been
concerned about my welfare and my children's safety. They
had witnessed a gradual change in my husband, as well, and
were uncertain about his decision making. Needless to say,
that weekend was a time of eye-opening revelation to me. The
speaker explained the signs of abusive behavior and the slow

unraveling of self-worth and empowerment. I saw the Lord's hand in giving me a loving sister who reached out and threw a lifeline to her drowning sibling.

Shortly after my sons and I were locked out of our home, Nathan became very ill with an asthma attack. With drastic physical changes in his life, and the emotional triggers that can exacerbate respiratory issues, it was heartbreaking to watch him struggle through this time. It was critical to get his asthma medication and our nebulizer machine to help him breathe easier. Unfortunately, all his medical supplies and medications were in our boarded-up home. I needed to get some bolt cutters to break the chains that kept us out and enlist the protection of our local police department to remove these essential medical items.

When the police car rolled up, I introduced myself to the young officer. As we walked up to the house, he began telling me of the night my husband called them to file a report. Oscar told them he had been a former sub rosa (undercover) officer for LAPD. He was adamant that I had kidnapped our sons, and he didn't know if they were dead or alive. He never mentioned that he had pulled out a 9mm weapon and waved it in front of me, telling me he was going to take care of me.

"The mouths of fools are their undoing, and their lips are a snare to their very lives" (Proverbs 18:7).

The pertinent questions of this rookie officer quickened my spirit to question the stories of my life with Oscar. Waves of insightful revelation poured over me like water. The curtain was being pulled back and another picture of my husband was becoming clear. I knew something was frighteningly wrong with what the officer was telling me—and all the stories I had heard throughout my marriage.

The young officer stated that he thought only the seasoned officers were able to work sub rosa. He further revealed that he had never heard of anyone being used to work undercover detail without finishing the Police Academy. Lastly, he was surprised that Oscar wanted to lock me out of our home. It is part of police training to know California community property laws in domestic-relations cases. It seemed as though the dark cloud was lifting, and the web of lies was beginning to untangle. My heart and mind were being prepared to handle more of the horrors this story would reveal.

My husband became my enemy and the person I wanted to protect my sons from. It was then that I researched his background and found out he was *never* employed by the Los Angeles Police Department. He had *never* been accepted to the Academy, though he regularly shared that he had with many in our family, church, and community. He had repeated the same lies to us throughout our fourteen-year marriage. With a great deal of sorrow and sadness, I sat down with my sons and let them know that the stories they had heard from their father were not true, and they would not be able to repeat them any longer. This was another huge loss for us to process. We were now forced to embrace our new life without him and hold on to what good memories we had.

> "LOVE AND PAIN ARE THE TWO CHAMBERS OF THE SAME HEART THAT PUMP COURAGE THROUGH THE ACHING VEINS" (ANN VOSKAMP).[2]

Rebecca and her husband graciously loaned me money to sustain us during this time. Words cannot express my gratitude and deep appreciation for their act of love and kindness. I filed for a legal separation and a restraining order to protect my sons and myself from further harm. Oscar countered with a divorce. This began the legal nightmare that would be an eye-opening education for the next several years.

Remarkably, this also began a journey of seeking God's magnificent hand in our lives as we moved in with my parents for over a year. The time with my mom and dad was the healing balm of many years of pent-up hurt and shame that I could not share with them earlier in my life. Their selflessness with the boys and I were visible examples of God's hand of provision, encouragement, and daily direction. I will never forget my father's words to us. He said, "I want you to know you are loved and you have a place to live safely, without fear."

This would begin a time, however difficult to walk through, with God going before us. We witnessed several miracles as the body of Christ reached out to feed, clothe, and pray for us. During that time, the Lord sustained me physically to work three and four jobs. This was necessary in order to remain current on my house payments even though I could not safely live there. I worked as the church secretary, did laundry for people, prepared meals for church families, and tutored students. Picking up extra work was always on my radar. It would help me pay another bill and stock our cupboards for another week. The eventual sale of my home would enable my sons and I to start over.

During that season another language emerged from my soul: the language of tears. Years of unprocessed grief were percolating through my veins. Only during the moments I was alone, driving to and from my many jobs, would the faucet flow. I wanted to be strong for my sons, who were facing their own heartbreak and trying to make sense of their upside-down lives. They fought with each other regularly from the anger and fear that gripped them. As much as possible, I would not put them in a position to carry my grief as well. It was a weight that I could barely manage myself.

One Mother's Day, my sons and I returned home from an enjoyable time at my sister's house. It was a long drive back home; we talked and laughed. Our emotional cups were filled up. When we walked in the door our phone's answering machine signal light was flashing. Isaac ran over to hear the message, hoping one of his friends had called. What we heard, instead, set my nerves on edge. It was the strong voice of a man identifying himself as a police officer who was looking for me. He said Oscar had gone to the police station to report me for violating a court order. Oscar told them I had deliberately taken my kids away from him on his visitation weekend. I was instructed to call the police station immediately.

Once again, fear and anxiety came over me. I mentally reviewed what I had done, if anything, to warrant this disturbing phone call. I clearly remembered discussing this visitation issue with Oscar before Mother's Day weekend to avoid any problems. It was documented in our divorce decree that, despite whoever's weekend it was to have the boys, Oscar would get them on Father's Day, and I would have them on Mother's Day. This was standard for most divorce custody agreements. Oscar knew this and had agreed ahead of time.

Immediately, upon receiving the Sergeant's message, I called the Police Station to discuss what had transpired regarding this Mother's Day weekend. He already knew of Oscar's name from all the times he had called to tell the police that I had stolen our children or violated a court order regarding his visitation rights. The Sergeant told me he couldn't give me any advice, but to document everything and get a good lawyer. Unfortunately, this was a disturbing end to an otherwise peaceful weekend.

Some of Isaac's weekend visits with his dad ended in arguments and him running away from his father's house. I remember, driving frantically over to get him while he was running down the road. At times, I felt so helpless in trying to console my sons from the pain inflicted by their father. This could only be done with lots of prayer and steady encouragement. I knew who their true healer was and prayed daily that God would heal the wounds inflicted on them through their dad and the horrors of divorce.

After the initial trauma of being locked out of our home and our lives being turned on their heads, Nathan developed some strange allergies. One day while I was working and he was in my sister Lynn's care, he had a reaction to some lunch she made. His face blew up around his eye and became red and swollen. He told her he felt funny and couldn't finish eating his hotdog with pork n' beans. When she turned around to look at him, his face was distorted like the Elephant Man. Thinking quick on her feet, she took him to Urgent Care. Nathan was given a steroid shot to quiet the growing itch and swelling.

This was the beginning of numerous appointments with doctors and specialists to determine the cause of the various food allergies. Nathan's allergic reactions were progressive and would quickly involve the swelling of his tongue and throat. This poor kid was pin-pricked like a porcupine. He needed to carry an EpiPen and Benadryl with him wherever he went.

Nathan would go through several difficult years of not being able to eat many varieties of beans, legumes, soy products, eggs, milk products, and wheat without having a reaction. The worst reaction came from any kind of bean, which resulted in his tongue and throat swelling and causing anaphylactic shock.

Life had become complicated, and sometimes overwhelmingly challenging, for Nathan and me. I tried to find things I could cook for him to keep him healthy. I was ordering spelt flour on the internet and trying to make him creative pizzas with rice milk cheese. Some of these newly invented food items were tasteless and uninviting. Most of my experiments were handled with laughter, but we were both frustrated with this new curveball to his diet.

Nathan definitely had his share of life's challenges as a young boy: abandoned by his Father, food allergies, learning disabilities, and cystic acne, all while navigating life as a hormonal teenager. How I wished and prayed he could be given a break from this heavy load. It had affected his academic work and school was becoming a mountainous challenge. Many mornings were met with his desire to stay home instead of facing another day of the overwhelming challenges at school.

After completing a series of academic tests from the school district's psychologists, Nathan was officially diagnosed with

Dyslexia and Attention Deficit Disorder (A.D.D.). I tried every homeopathic remedy I could find: Omega 3 Vitamins for the brain; cross lateral body exercises; half a cup of regular coffee with half a cup of non-dairy milk; more sports activity; special tapping techniques to rewire the brain. Nothing seemed to have any lasting effect.

Finally, after numerous complaints from his teachers and his inability to complete his in-class assignments, I agreed to put him on Concerta, a commonly used drug for those with Attention Deficit Disorder. Change was immediate. By the end of that week, his teacher told me he had completed a math assignment with the rest of the class. What used to take him two hours to complete, he was able to finish in 30 minutes. Victory was on the horizon.

Within weeks, Nathan dropped a significant amount of weight and had no appetite. He lost over 25 pounds and barely ate. This was a side-effect of the drug. His normal gregarious laughter, fun personality, and sharp wit were no longer a part of our home. He was disappearing before my eyes. He would sit quietly while Isaac and I would engage in conversation. Something drastic was happening to my son. I felt like we were losing him. Nathan told me the medication made him feel different, not like himself, and he was really sad about it. We changed to another medication but the side-effects of that new drug caused depression and possible suicide. That option was off the table, as well. Nathan and I decided he wouldn't take another drug that changed the wonderfully engaging person God made him to be.

One of the bravest and most difficult times was when he joined the football team in high school. He was big, brawny, and athletically capable. That combination alone would give you the confidence to stand tall and join the team. But the food allergies, asthma, learning challenges, and emotional issues with his father were a constant deterrent to getting where he wanted to go. The combination of all these obstacles were hard enough for a well-equipped adult, let alone for a young teen-ager navigating his way through some very turbulent waters.

One day during his freshman year, he called me from school because his throat was closing up due to the toxins from the smell of beans they were cooking in the school cafeteria. After hearing the fear in his voice, I knew we had turned a corner on his ability to stay at school. Given the school's small configuration, there was no way he could get to his classes without passing by the cafeteria. We, of course, could not control what they cooked on any given day.

For the next semester, Nathan was on independent study. He felt isolated from friends and the structure of school. Depression and lack of motivation encircled him. We eventually had to move to a different city where he could attend a larger school. In this new campus, Nathan didn't have to pass by the cafeteria on the way to class and risk the horror of anaphylactic shock to his system. It was there he would join another football team and be able to participate for a season in the sport he loved.

Every Thursday before the Friday football game, the team moms delivered a delicious catered lunch to the players to get them pumped up. They had decided to serve enchilada casserole with beans. Nathan didn't want to miss it for fear of ridicule by ruthless teammates. I told him I would bring him some food that he could eat, and he could join his team from a far table. I watched him sit alone eating his healthy food bar, though he couldn't enjoy the laughter and camaraderie with the players.

Although not what he wanted, he was willing to do what was necessary to be part of the team and not miss this lunch. I was so proud of his effort and his refusal to give up. I felt helpless that I couldn't fix this overwhelming food issue. It had caused Nathan so much fear, inconvenience, and discomfort. He had to constantly find ways to work around his dietary needs yet still remain connected to the things he wanted to do.

Once while strolling down the aisles at Whole Foods trying to find some expensive flour I could use to bake Nathan something he craved, I saw him reading the ingredients on all the chips packages. Chips were one of his favorite things to indulge in. He looked up at me with water filled eyes and said, "God must really hate me, Mom; I can't eat any of the things I love." My heart sank as I tried to quickly refute that statement. As time went on, doctors and specialists became more common in our schedule. I saw courage and determination rise up in him as he slowly, and painfully, embraced the challenges he was given.

7

THE MIRACLES

If the Lord be with us, we have no cause of fear. His eye
is upon us, His arm over us, His ear open to our prayer
- His grace sufficient, His promise unchangeable.

—John Newton[1]

One night I was driving to my parents' home after working a long day. I had been crying out to the Lord while tears streamed down my face asking Him to show me how I could earn an additional seven hundred dollars. I needed to pay the mortgage so I wouldn't lose my house. Already working all the hours I could manage, I didn't know how I could possibly find more time to work another job. Things were critical since Oscar refused to help me make the house payments after walking away from our marriage.

Discouraged and exhausted, I walked up the steps to the front door. On the top step I saw a small brown box that was addressed to me but had no return address. Lynn was at the house watching the boys, and I asked her if she had seen anyone drop off this box. She said she had been at the house for several hours but had not heard anyone drive by. Surprisingly, she also said there was no box there when she entered the house. I walked into the kitchen and started to open the unexpected package when I began to see several large bills lining the bottom of the box. The amount was $700 exactly—precisely the amount I needed to pay my mortgage on time. My God had supplied my need! And I was able to stay current on my house payment. To this day, I never found out how that money got there. It provided a way to make my mortgage payment and keep my home so my sons and I could start over.

During my marriage, Rebecca had given me a lovely entertainment center for our living room. I really loved this thoughtful gift from her and used it to display my family pictures. It was made of beautiful walnut wood and was the perfect fit for my home. When the time came to empty my house so I could sell it, I reluctantly gave away the entertainment center because I didn't have the money to store it. This was another loss of something important to me—something I really valued but couldn't hang onto.

After living with my parents for a year and a half, I heard of a rental home for my sons and me. Upon entering house, there was a lovely entertainment center inside, against the wall, exactly like the one my sister had given me. Touched by this sign of familiarity, I stepped forward to read a note attached that said, "use this for as long as you need." The fingerprints of the Lord were on that home, including an identical piece of furniture that I had been forced to give up. It brought comfort to my heart. It was the Lord's way of telling me He knew my every heartache, and He was there to meet all of our needs.

"Lean on, trust in, and be confident in the Lord with all your heart and mind and do not rely on your own insight or understanding. In all your ways know, recognize, and acknowledge Him and He will direct and make straight and plain your paths" (Proverbs 3:5-6, Amplified Bible, Classic Edition).

Given all the emotional and physical changes in our lives: living out of suitcases, mandatory court-ordered counseling for the boys, and working several jobs, car repairs were low on my list of priorities. My brakes would scream at me every time I went around a corner on our mountain roads. A sweet couple at church, Mike and Susie, asked me how I was managing all the changes in my life. My car came up in the conversation. The concerned look on their faces told me I needed to prioritize my screaming brakes as soon as possible. I didn't have the extra money to pay for this expense. Turning to the Lord, once again, I prayed for more work. A few days later I received a check in the mail with more than enough to cover the bill for my brakes and even new tires! God was definitely my provider—He was the husband I needed to take care of the things I required.

New winter jackets for the boys were provided by an older couple, Art and Carol, from our church. They had watched and prayed while much of the saga was unfolding in our lives; waiting to see how they could meet a need. Watching my sons grow taller and their jackets shorter was their perfect opportunity to step in with loving kindness. Bags of clothes were given to me with gently used professional attire I badly needed for work. I had lost over forty pounds from all the stress of my surgeries, crumbling marriage, and long hours worked. Hardly any of my clothes fit me anymore. I was in need of so many things, but I wasn't comfortable asking for them. God provided in abundance, even things I would never think of asking for were included in these bags: comfortable shoes, stylish purses, and undergarments that were my perfect size.

"And my God will meet all your needs according to the riches of His Glory in Christ Jesus" (Philippians 4:19).

Both of my sons were involved in a theatrical mime group. The group presented patriotic songs using American Sign Language and drama. One weekend the devoted families of this young theatrical group gleaned their closets, garages, and homes to orchestrate a large garage sale on our behalf. After tirelessly serving at the all-day yard sale, they came over to present us with a beautiful card filled with a large stack of money, proceeds of their efforts. This outpouring of love and concern for our difficult situation left an indelible memory of God's love through the kindness of others.

"Carry each other's burdens, and in this way you will fulfill the law of Christ" (Galatians 6:2).

One of the hardest things for me was working endless hours to pay for the home that was not safe to live in. I needed my half of the equity from this house. Desperately, I tried to sell it so I could pay my bills. I needed the money from our home to care for my sons. But Oscar thwarted every effort to sell our home. He would not accept any reasonable offers we received from eager buyers. As an act of control, he refused to sign paperwork for the sale of our home, even after he had agreed to sell it.

Discouraged by Oscar's cruel manipulation, I learned that no judge or legal order can make you sign something if you refuse to do it. Our judicial system—the court—was definitely my last resort in this nightmare I was living. No one could require Oscar to act honorably or provide for his family. Only God could, and would, reveal himself through this season of desperation.

One day after praying in anguish to the Lord, I called my attorney's secretary. She was a believer, and I asked her to pray that Oscar would agree to sell our home. I needed to pay my attorney's fees and other expenses. She told me that Oscar's attorney was one of the rudest and most difficult people they had ever dealt with. He had that reputation among the family law attorneys and was proud of it. Acting highly unprofessional, he did not return their phone calls or respond in a timely manner to legal correspondence. He bullied other attorneys, and he looked in disgust at me in the courtroom.

Her voice told me she wasn't hopeful that any changes would happen soon.

Later that afternoon, I received an unexpected call from her asking me if I was sitting down. She excitedly told me that my attorney had been surprised at court that day. Oscar's attorney was carrying paperwork; Oscar was finally willing to sell our home. He said Oscar wanted to buy a Harley Davidson Motorcycle and was now ready to sell the house. Even through material greed, the Lord provided a way for our house to be sold. The equity money from the sale of our home was to be equally distributed between us.

"And without faith it is impossible to please God, because anyone who comes to him must believe that he exists and that he rewards those who earnestly seek him" (Hebrews 11:6).

During the early years of raising our sons, I taught classes to homeschool families. One family in particular had several children with learning challenges. These children struggled with reading, comprehension, and writing. After the parents found out my marriage had ended they offered me a job as a tutor in the center they were opening in a nearby town. They provided the training. I worked hard teaching, managing, and building their business. It was a win-win for both parties.

However, the long hours away from home were taking their toll and both my sons were struggling. They had faced a formidable loss without their father in their lives, and now they rarely saw me due to the extensive hours required by my job. This was made worse by my long commute. They needed my help with homework, relationships, emotional and moral support. My parents were exhausted from helping me parent and keeping my family together while I was away working.

I was deeply grateful for the valuable opportunity and work I had been given but was torn knowing my sons were struggling with their daily responsibilities. Feeling pulled to be the responsible provider was tearing me up because I wanted to be near my children. Once again, I prayed that the Lord would open up a way so I could work out of my home and provide for my first ministry: taking care of my sons. He did exactly that.

The skills I learned as a Certified Professional Tutor would enable me to provide a living for my boys and develop a reputable tutoring business. Only God knew I would need to work out of my home someday as my sons grew up and needed me to be closer to home. The Lord provided training and compassion for me to teach children with learning differences like my own. He had changed my arena and advocacy to work with children and their families without an advocate. One by one, He brought me wonderful families to work with. God also clearly revealed to me the truth of my own struggles with learning challenges.

Friends from our home-schooled group rallied around us. They continually offered their prayers and support. Some asked if I would tutor their children. This work provided enough money to pay a constant flow of attorney's bills. I was working hard to press through this distorted picture of what life had become. Being able to have meaningful work to support my sons and myself was rewarding. This gave me the confidence to believe that the Lord was with me through every new challenge.

Isaac had been invited to spend some time with a friend he had grown up with. His mother, Traci, was a supportive friend. She and her husband had witnessed the changes in my marriage. They were there with words of encouragement and offered to have Isaac over to spend time with their family. On this particular day, I was emotionally and physically exhausted. Traci asked me how I was doing. I was trying very hard to hold back the tears, but the dam broke. She held me while I cried and put a check for one hundred dollars in my hand with a note. It said, "This is for you and the boys to do something special." I saved her precious note in my wallet for years. It also read, "You *will* get through this!"

Another God-given friend was Becky. Having four boys of her own, she had hired me to work with her oldest son. After the tutoring sessions she would walk me to my car. She patiently listened to the continuing saga of court hearings and schemes Oscar initiated. Although her husband was a well-educated man, he worked for a Christian college and earned a third of what he could have made at a public institution. They had budgeted carefully and were able to give me a check to pay for the various needs my boys had for clothes, sports, and food.

Before going to work one day, a sweet friend named Judy called to meet me for breakfast. As a pastor's wife she always had wonderful words of encouragement from the Bible to share with me. True to her character, she told me about Isaiah 43 and presented me with a small silk bird as a reminder that His eye is on the sparrow and His eye was on me too. It was a simple and yet profound reminder of the Lord's tender love for me and my sons. As a comforting reminder, I kept that little bird on my window seal for years.

There was a wonderful elderly couple who were a terrific example of godly living: The Frankamps. They volunteered a few months out of every year to work for Habitat for Humanity. Cheerfully, they worked alongside college students building homes for the needy. They also had a wood ministry in our community. Remarkably, they both chopped dead trees providing wood to widows and single moms needing to warm their homes during the cold winter months. They had invested their money wisely and owned a few homes in our neighborhood which they rented to people who had come upon hard times. Through them the Lord miraculously provided a lovely home for my sons and me. It was a safe place to rebuild our lives.

I continued to work several jobs to pay for the growing expenses with the boys' needs, car repairs, and attorney's fees.

During the winter season, I caught a severe upper respiratory infection that turned into Asthma. I was struggling to shake this infection and was laid up for a few weeks. My doctor gave me strict instructions to rest due to the seriousness of the infection or he would put me in the hospital. Reluctantly, I listened to his advice but was physically unable to fulfill my duties as the church secretary. This was a large part of my income. The Frankamps noticed my absence and inquired about my circumstances. They graciously called me and told me they were gifting me one month's rent so I could get on my feet financially after missing work.

God answered my prayers specifically providing a home to rent that I would eventually buy from the Frankamps. It even had an extra room for an office to enable me to tutor out of my home. I saw God's hand release the funds from the sale of my former house at exactly the right time to put a down payment on a new home. When we moved into this place, God furnished it with a generous supply of donations. Our church heard we needed beds, linens, couches, dishes, and a file cabinet for my home office. Everything we needed was generously provided at just the right time.

One of the greatest gifts from the Lord during this time, in addition to my family, was a wonderful friend named Linda East. She was kind, gracious, and generous. I met her at a women's luncheon where she was giving her testimony about the loss of her only adult son who had been a youth pastor. Dan was killed in an automobile accident on his way to set up a large church event combining three youth groups. This tragedy was compounded by the fact that he and his lovely wife had just adopted three children from a Russian orphanage. They already had a nine-year-old son and a three-month-old baby girl. It was such a devastating loss for his family, his church, and all those his life impacted. Linda and her husband, Kurt, were faithful to provide emotional and financial support to their daughter-in-law and five grandchildren.

After I moved into my house, Linda came by to see how I was doing. She noticed I didn't have appropriate bed linens for my bedroom. I had used left-over blankets after setting up the boys' rooms. She told me she had to go pick up something and would be back later. Linda went home, took off the bedding in her guest room, and came back with a beautiful feminine comforter, Battenberg lace pillows, and shams to dress up my shabby room. She told me I deserved to have a room to come home to that looked pretty and relaxing. Caring and giving, she held a weekly Bible study in her home where she ministered to six or eight of us on a regular basis. Although she was still processing her own grief, she reached out to show the love of Christ to others experiencing pain. She listened carefully and wiped away my tears as I cried through those turbulent months of abandonment, betrayal and numerous court appearances. God was showing His love to me in so many ways through the meeting of our physical, emotional, and spiritual needs.

"A FRIEND LOVES AT ALL TIMES" (PROVERBS 17:17).

All of this was rather miraculous since I had given all my furniture away to a friend and mom with seven children. I did this in an act of desperation since I didn't have the money to store my furniture and she needed all the items that were offered. My friend took the seats out of her broken-down van and brought her two oldest children to help her carry several loads of blankets, dishes, pots and pans, tables, beds, a dining room set, and couches. After several trips back and forth from my house to hers, she was able to empty my home and have all the items she needed to care for her large family. God provided for her needs and mine. My home became empty so it could be sold.

There was a man named Mike who lived next door to my parents. He was a music professor at a local college and had asked me several times to go out on a date. I turned him down letting him know I wasn't interested in dating anyone and that my priority was caring for my sons. He would offer my boys small jobs like moving wood from his deck to the inside of his home, pulling weeds, and raking his yard. He was gently persistent, but I remained steadfast in not wanting to complicate my life by dating someone at that time.

The week I moved into our new home, Mike was refinishing a mosaic table for his living room when he had a heart attack. He leaned over his table and died. His family flew in from New York to handle the probate arrangements. They had heard about me from Mike and asked my parents to have me come over prior to their scheduled probate sale and pick out anything the boys and I needed. I was so grateful for their generous offer and was able to get a washing machine, a dryer, a bed for my son, a roll-top desk for my office, dishes, furniture, gorgeous plants, and even canisters filled with flour all ready for baking. Although I never dated Mike, he helped furnish my home.

"And my God will meet all your needs according to the riches of his glory in Christ Jesus" (Philippians 4:19).

Shortly after my sons and me were settling into our new place, two thoughtful friends decided to give us a housewarming party. Jessica and Kathy truly blessed us with their kindness in celebrating this new season of our lives. Several friends who had supported us during the upheaval of our family were invited. These two tender hearted ladies brought food, drinks, and gifts. Without asking for anything, they set-up and cleaned up everything so I would not have any added responsibilities. They were the hands and feet of Christ right in our home.

Three years after my divorce, I was still paying several thousands of dollars to my attorney to represent me in court due to the continued emotional abuse to my sons. We needed supervised visitations, court-ordered counseling for the boys, and anger management classes for their father. He constantly tried to find loopholes to get out of paying his legally required child support.

"He upholds the cause of the oppressed and gives food to the hungry, The Lord sets the prisoners free, the Lord gives sight to the blind, the Lord lifts up those who are bowed down, the Lord loves the righteous. . . and sustains the Fatherless and the widow, but he frustrates the ways of the wicked" (Psalm 146:7-9).

Oscar never tired of looking for ways to destroy me financially, emotionally, and spiritually. He would intentionally put the wrong address on my child support check so it would be returned to him. Then he would delay it another week or two before resending it with a fake note saying he made a *mistake*. By God's intervention, he never won any of the legal claims he put forth. He was so frustrated with judgements in my favor that he even asked my attorney why he was never victorious in court. He was told that his claims were unjust and he should give up trying. He never did.

"But you, Lord, are a shield around me, my glory, the One who lifts my head high" (Psalm 3:3).

The slow erosion of Oscar's heart toward me and our family was difficult to absorb but the physical changes in his appearance were equally as challenging to process. He adopted the look of a biker with a do-rag on his head, beer belly, leather jacket, and cow's testicles hanging from the tailgate of his truck. His face was angry; his voice was harsh; and a negative attitude of cynicism permeated most conversations. It was as though the kind, funny personality, and laughter that originally attracted me to him had moved out and a troubled, mean-spirited man was now living inside of him.

Looking back, I could see so many hidden signs that I was never looking for. Although Oscar had done a good job of hiding most of the clues, I did find out later that his father had been abusive to him and found ample opportunity to demean him publicly. Years later, I learned from my mother-in-law that Oscar was always getting in trouble at school. He sought attention through negative behavior and shock value. He was expelled for blowing up a vending machine and for arguing with a teacher. Although smart and cunning, he used it to fool and deceive those unsuspecting people around him.

My life was just the opposite. I was a steady plotter and didn't take many risks. I was afraid of making mistakes and disappointing those around me. Honor and respect were paramount in my culture and home life. I worked hard at being dependable and honest, afraid to shame myself or my family. Loyalty and dependability were the hallmarks of my framework. Oscar and I were like oil and water. I now see why it was important for him to align himself with someone like me—to give credibility around the illusions he lived.

Oscar had created a life of past honorable accomplishments that would make any mother proud. The regrettable reality, though, was they were not true. He kept many who loved him in the dark of ever really knowing who he was. His protective hedge of false stories kept family and friends at arms' length and from any true intimacy of relationship. No one could get beyond the lies to discover the real Oscar.

He was smart and mechanically gifted, but he wasn't satisfied with working with his hands. His father once told me he believed Oscar was the most technically gifted of his three sons. He was intelligent, mechanically savvy, and had a keen mind for facts and figures. His potential was unlimited. As an immigrant coming to the United States through Ellis Island with little money and the hope of rare opportunities, my father-in-law had high hopes for each of his children. It was evident Oscar's father was disappointed that his talented son hadn't made better choices to achieve more in life.

"For all that is secret will eventually be brought into the open, and everything that is concealed will be brought to light and made known to all" (Luke 8:17, NLT).

8

RESTORATION AND HEALING

God has been good and He will continue to manifest His goodness. Let us approach these days expecting to see the goodness of the Lord manifest. Let us be strong and of good courage, for the Lord will fight for us if we stand in faith.

—Francis Frangipane[1]

After three years of this dark and sometimes desperate season, the Lord brought a wonderful godly man into my life named Paul. We met on a Christian online dating service. I was encouraged by my kind-hearted friend, Heather, who noticed my life was out of balance.

She said, "All you do is work, work, work and take care of your boys and your parents."

I told her, "I thought that was my life."

She said, "You need a balance; some friends to have dinner with and adults to talk to. Come and try out this reputable Christian dating service."

Privately, I was grateful for her prodding. Someone had noticed what I needed, while I was too busy on the treadmill of life to see it myself.

We drove down together to the Christian dating service. I paid my money, showed my divorce paperwork, had my picture taken, and filled out some forms about my statement of faith. They gave me a password to access their website and we were on our way to have lunch to celebrate this new chapter in my life. Heather was excited for me. She wanted me to have some good quality friendships and some evenness to my bumpy, hectic, schedule. I was cautiously excited but afraid at the same time. I didn't want to enter another bad relationship. And I definitely didn't want to cause any more pain for my sons. I would take baby steps and proceed with caution.

With controlled excitement, I reviewed several online biographies, poured over pictures, and read the reasons these potential dates were looking for a relationship. Hardly any of them described how they came to know Christ and the importance He had in their lives. Most were looking for someone to replace the void in their pursuits and distract them from their emptiness. One nice looking man bragged about the amount of money he had. He would even be willing to use it on the *right person* who desired plastic surgery for a better body. This was sadly laughable. Worldly perspectives had not skipped over the Christian dating service.

The only one who seemed to take this whole dating-after-marriage process seriously was Paul. He had a handsome smile and wore a nice sports coat in his picture. Proudly, he wrote about his two adult children and his efforts to maintain a consistent relationship with them, despite the divorce from their mother.

I sent Paul an introductory email to say hello, and he responded quickly. He surprisingly told me that he had discontinued his membership with the dating service after a five-year membership. Somehow my email got through to him. We began corresponding with daily emails, and soon he was calling me every night after my boys were in bed. While I was still working in my office, we talked about our kids, jobs, hobbies and what we wanted in a future relationship.

On our first date, Paul met me for lunch at Mimi's, and we talked for several hours. I told him I had to leave to buy groceries and pick up my boys. He surprised me by telling me he had a present for me in his car. Since it was a really hot day, I figured any chocolate he might have bought was melted on his car seat or if he bought me flowers, they were wilted by now. But instead, he had remembered I needed to buy groceries, and he went to a Farmers Market before our lunch date to buy me three shopping bags of fresh produce.

Wow! Was I impressed! But that was not all. He had listened to me, in our evening telephone conversations, about my concerns regarding my younger son's reading challenges. He held up his own series of *The Chronicles of Narnia* and said, "I heard you when you said your son was struggling with reading so I'm loaning you my own set of books and you can read them together. Boys need adventure."

Nathan and I would sit together at night. I would read these great stories and he would listen. To my surprise, he enjoyed them. Shortly after, *The Chronicles of Narnia* was made into a movie and Paul bought us VIP tickets at the El Capitan Theatre in Hollywood for the film's debut. The theatre stage was like a movie set with props and scenery from the movie. We had great seats, free popcorn, and VIP special cups with our sodas. It was a great time seeing a spectacular movie we could all enjoy and some of Hollywood's eccentricities.

For the first time in my life, I began to learn what a normal, healthy, respectable, relationship looked like. Paul was even-tempered and consistent in his respect for my sons and me. He listened to their interests and bought them things he thought they would enjoy. We began the process of learning about each other and discovered our life paths had been similar in upbringing, betrayal, and abandonment.

Paul courted me for a year before we married. He wanted to attend church with us when he came to visit, but the distance between our homes was over a hundred miles, so it was difficult to drive back and forth. Paul decided to speak to the boys individually. He asked them if he could sleep in my office so we could attend church together on Sundays. It was good for my sons to see how a woman is treated respectfully in a relationship. They both agreed but didn't understand why he was doing this when their friends' mothers had boyfriends who would sleep in their moms' bedrooms. Paul explained to them that this was not honoring to me, and it was not biblical. This would be a new healthy male role model for them.

Paul proposed to me on a gondola ride in Naples, California. Peacefully, we floated through the canals listening to our gondola driver singing songs in Italian. A basket of bread, cheese, and a bottle of wine were provided for the romantic sunset cruise. It was there that Paul pulled out a beautiful emerald and diamond engagement ring and asked if I would marry him. I cheerfully replied, "Yes, I will." The preparation began for a wedding and a new life filled with hope.

Our marriage verse would be: **"Now to him who is able to do immeasurably more than all we can ask or imagine, according to his power that is at work within us, to Him be Glory in the church and in Christ Jesus, for ever and ever! Amen." (Ephesians 3:20).**

God had brought me my Boaz. He is not a perfect man, but through his own heartaches and disappointments, he has been refined by the refiner's fire. We continue to work through issues of life with adult children, blended families, retirement, aging parents, and our own health concerns.

During the first decade of our marriage we attended a thriving church in Santa Clarita, California called The Sanctuary (www.thesanctuarychurch.com). They offered Life Groups consisting of twelve-week classes to help connect the members in a more intimate area of specific interest. We attended a *Communication in Marriage* class by Emerson Eggerichs (www. loveandrespect.com). There we met several other blended families and learned foundational skills on how to effectively communicate through the trials of marriage.

From a series of conversations initiated in this class, I was approached by a pastor at our church who asked if I would be interested in being a representative of the church for the Santa Clarita Valley Pregnancy Center (www.scvpc.org). I soon found out that this dynamic church is a strong supporter of the transforming work of SCVPC. I felt compelled to volunteer and come alongside young girls facing the same crisis in pregnancy I had experienced. I wanted to be a voice for the life-long consequences to their decision and offer to assist in any capacity necessary.

The President/CEO, Angela Bennett, (www.angelabennett. org) conducted an interview with me to become a volunteer at the pregnancy center and was perceptive in asking if I had ever taken a post-abortion class to process my grief. Little did I know how pivotal this twelve-week class would be in healing the forty years of scars from my abortion. How I wished this center had been available to me decades earlier. After volunteering for several months at this valuable community resource, I would become a staff member, working as a case manager.

"Lord you alone are my portion and my cup; you have made my lot secure. The boundary lines have fallen for me in pleasant places; surely I have a delightful inheritance" (Psalm 16:5,6).

This experience was divinely directed. I was finally in a safe marriage with the loving support to uncover the deep hurt and loss of my fallen babies. The post-abortion class also gave me the opportunity to process my loss through the miscarriage I had in between my two sons—a life event that was buried under the stress and trauma of a turbulent marriage. I was now able to look at these experiences with a new attitude, and more parts of the puzzle emerged. There were many factors I had never considered that contributed to my decision to agree to an abortion. Willingly, I had taken all the blame on myself and it added to my shame.

Roe vs. Wade, the 1973 United States Supreme Court decision legalizing abortion, had just been passed the year before I stepped into that abortion clinic. There was a tidal wave of support from women and men believing this was the road to freedom of *choice* following the sexual revolution sweeping our country. Broken from the years of childhood sexual abuse and without my boyfriend's support, having a child alone was too high a mountain for me to climb. I didn't have the self-confidence or the community of support I needed to forge through the idea of being a single mother and raising a baby alone. Shame still plagued my decision at least in my mind, and in my current immature emotional capabilities, there was no way out except through those clinic doors.

Today it's a different story. With compassionate workers at crisis pregnancy centers throughout the U.S., women and men are being educated on the medical science of what takes place in their bodies. They are offered free pregnancy tests and ultrasounds, at medically certified pregnancy centers, that allow them to actually see the life growing within them. On the ultrasound screen, a pulsating, human heartbeat is visible at six weeks of life, as are the tiny hands and feet moving around in the amniotic fluid. Compassionate support by trained case managers and life skills classes are available both during and after the pregnancy. Additionally, many pregnancy centers provide practical items for their clients, such as, diapers, baby clothes, blankets, diaper bags, etc. Today, we are living in a different cultural time of awareness regarding the true *choices* for women and men about a life they conceived and the responsibility of becoming parents.

The post-abortion class was a safe and loving place, providing a comprehensive way to learn about everything that influenced my decision. Surprisingly, I also learned why the medical procedure that followed my miscarriage twenty years later brought back so many memories of smells, sounds, and emotional trauma related to my abortion. The tragedy of losing a child through miscarriage was a physical and emotional trigger that ignited long-suppressed feelings. Now, with a fresh pair of eyes and a new heart, I could see the circumstances differently. The Word of God was a healing salve that revealed His wonderful forgiveness to me and to the others who have walked this road of abortion. Knowing that my Lord and Savior suffered and died on a cross for my sins gave this sin of abortion a new perspective.

> TODAY, WE ARE LIVING IN A DIFFERENT CULTURAL TIME OF AWARENESS REGARDING THE TRUE *CHOICES* FOR WOMEN AND MEN ABOUT A LIFE THEY CONCEIVED AND THE RESPONSIBILITY OF BECOMING PARENTS.

"Therefore, there is now no condemnation for those who are in Christ Jesus" (Romans 8:1).

Paul and I had the opportunity to attend a Care Net conference while I worked at the Santa Clarita Valley Pregnancy Center. Care Net is a vital support organization for life-affirming crisis pregnancy centers throughout America. Its focus is sharing the Gospel of Jesus Christ and strengthening families through marriage, parenting, and adoption. They maintain a real-time pregnancy decision call center. Care Net provides education, coaching, and annual conferences throughout the United States. They encourage and educate pregnancy centers regarding changing policies, legislation, and new technology to better support the life-changing work they do. We both were excited to see these changes taking place, especially in a Christian context.

The keynote speaker for the evening was Steve Arterburn. He is the founder and chairman of *New Life Ministries* (www. Newlife.com), and the host of the syndicated Christian counseling talk show, *New Life Live*. Steve has authored several books on sexual addiction and how to gain victory over addictive behavior. Among other important things, he spoke about his personal testimony of getting his girlfriend pregnant in college and then insisting she get an abortion. I was emotionally moved to tears when he sincerely apologized to all the post-abortive women in that large convention center who had never received an apology. It was truly the first time I had ever heard a man apologize for pushing someone into having an abortion. It touched a hidden place buried inside of me and peeled back another layer of healing.

The women I worked with at the Santa Clarita Valley Pregnancy Center who shared their stories of pain and heartache gave me the courage to press on. I trained to become a post-abortion counselor, teaching a twelve-week Bible study on healing the hurts from abortion. These women and me share an unbroken bond of loss and healing.

I have also been blessed with a group of women from Santa Clarita whom I deeply cherish: Diane B., Jeanette, Diane S., Kari, Kristine, Linda D., Judy, Darlene, Denise, and Deborah. Additionally, the wonderful women at *Tuesday with Friends*, Adel, Deanie, Debra, Gail, Babette, Sarah, Linda, Pam, Cookie, and Kristi, were my cheerleaders when I didn't know I had a story to tell. They listened, encouraged, and also reminded me of the power of a story. We all have a story to share, and they believed before I did that mine would benefit someone experiencing my former circumstances.

Effectively written, Stacy Eldridge explains the strength and value of female friendships very clearly in her book, *Captivating*.[2] These benefits are equally available to men in male friendships. She states:

Women need women friends. There is no way that a husband or children can provide the intimacy and relational satisfaction you need as a woman. A woman MUST have women friends. "There is a fierce jealousy, a fiery devotion, and a great loyalty between women friends. Our friendships flow in the deep waters of the heart where God dwells and transformation takes place. It is here, in this holy place, that a woman can partner with God and in impacting another and be impacted by another for lasting good. It is here that she can mother, nurture, encourage and call forth life.

Through the powerful transformation in my heart by the Love of God and the timely encouragement of these uniquely placed friends, I was able to look back with eyes of forgiveness and look forward with eyes of great hope. This is my prayer for you, precious reader, as you seek wisdom and boldness, to share your own testimony.

"They triumphed over him by the blood of the lamb and by the word of their testimony" (Revelation 12:11).

9

RECOGNIZING THE LOSS

*Death is not the greatest loss in life. The greatest
loss is what dies inside us while we live.*

—Norman Cousins[1]

A neighboring church, Grace Baptist (www.gracebaptist.
org/care), also provided community outreach and
offered a revealing class for women who had suffered
from childhood sexual abuse. The class was led by Wendy
McHaddad, a tender-hearted, clearly insightful woman who
had walked through the torment of her own sexual abuse.
We used Dr. Dan Allender's book and workbook, *Wounded
Heart—Hope for Adult Victims of Childhood Sexual Abuse.*
Weekly, we sifted through our difficult memories and the
choices we made in order to cope. Each one of us told our
story. It was there that I would see with the help and input
from others how this life-changing experience had altered my
thinking. Gratefully, my eyes were opened to see it through
the lens of the forgiveness of a loving God. I finally dismissed

any guilt and shame I carried from the self-imposed lie that the abuse was my fault.

This group of women would become my tribe of encouragement and inspiration, allowing me to continue to press forward and complete the class. There were similarities among us that reflect the statistics below. Several of us knew our abusers from our family or people that were acquaintances. Very few of us in this class were sexually abused by strangers. We also discovered that there was a deliberate plan by the perpetrators to set up the abusive situation. Understanding the process of abuse freed me from assuming unnecessary guilt for my compliance as a frightened child. It also helped me understand the events that evoked confusion and contempt when I was faced with similar circumstances.

In this group, we were able to be vulnerable and raw regarding our stories and feelings toward our perpetrators. This was something I had not experienced before. Vulnerability had always been a sign of weakness for me. I thought it showed a part of me that was unprepared for the challenges of life. It was too close to my real authentic self, and I stayed away from it.

Dr. Brené Brown, in her book, *Daring Greatly, How the Courage to Be Vulnerable Transforms the Way We Live, Love, Parent, and Lead,*[2] explains vulnerability like this:

> Vulnerability isn't good or bad: It's not what we call a dark emotion, nor is it always a light, positive experience. Vulnerability is the core of all emotions and feelings. To feel is to be vulnerable. To believe vulnerability is weakness is to believe that feeling is weakness. To foreclose on our emotional life out of a fear that the costs will be too high is to walk away from the very thing that gives purpose and meaning to living.
>
> Our rejection of vulnerability often stems from our associating it with dark emotions like fear, shame, grief, sadness

and disappointment—emotions that we don't want to discuss even when they profoundly affect the way we live,
work, and even lead. What most of us fail to understand
and what took me a decade of research to learn is that
vulnerability is also the cradle of the emotions and experiences that we crave. Vulnerability is the birthplace of love,
belonging, joy, courage, empathy, and creativity. It is the
source of hope, empathy, accountability, and authenticity.
If we want greater clarity in our purpose or deeper and
more meaningful spiritual lives, vulnerability is the path.

Dr. Brown's insight into vulnerability would prove true
within the stories and conversations in this group. We felt
deep compassion for one another and grew closer through
our vulnerability with each other. I began to trust the group
enough to share my shame and anger in ways I never knew I
carried it. This built a bridge of uncommon trust and acceptance with each person brave enough to commit to our weekly
meetings. It ultimately gave way to joy, courage, and empathy
for one another.

Specific characteristics flowed through this group of brave
women. Fear, shame, helplessness, betrayal, confusion, ambiva-
lence, loneliness, depression, anger, despair, secrecy, emptiness,
self-contempt, turbulent marriages, denial, inability to trust,
and a river of rage were common denominators among the
tribe. We learned that the issues found in all our lives were
more intense and dramatic due to a soul-hunger of victims of
sexual abuse. Our determination to push ahead in life, despite
the odds, would begin to involve an unpredictable cycle of
pain and contempt. The pain had become our enemy and
whoever was responsible for causing it.

Many struggled with overeating as a way of coping with
their internal anger and confusion. Some turned to drugs or
alcohol to forget for a limited time. We found comfort in
finally being able to share our struggles with someone who

truly understood our journey; someone who had walked this road of secrecy and shame but now provided heartfelt compassion and insight. We were mirrors for each other and could see the unnecessary, self-imposed guilt and shame embraced by the other more clearly than our own.

To look at this group of talented, successful women was deceiving. Each of us had pressed on with our lives to become wives, mothers, and professionals functioning in a competitive world. None of the underlying fractures from our past were evident when you looked at our carefully prepared and polished exteriors. In Dr. Allender's[3] comprehensive book, Wounded Heart, he explains this phenomenon well:

> Sexual abuse exacts a terrible price in the victim's life in terms of shame, contempt, and denial. The sins of the perpetrator continue to color the victim's life through an inability to enjoy relationship, intimacy, and hope. The victim's soul feels bound to denial; the heart feels wounded and alone. Longing for more or delighting in what is available equally stir and endanger the soul; therefore, the person feels it is better to live without awareness of passion, hunger or pain.

> This ache cannot be acknowledged, but neither can it be entirely silenced. The silent scream deepens and the paradox of living life without feeling in order to keep the threads of hope intact. The complex web of desire and defense, of longing and contempt, are often hidden below a socially competent exterior that does not look wounded or confused. The outwardly pleasant layer functions to control both the inner emptiness and shame and the risk in being deeply involved in relationship.

One of our soul-searching assignments was to tell our story by creating a collage poster of our younger self, using magazine pictures and printed words. On the other side of the poster, we were to create another collage to reveal who we are now and who we wanted to become. My finished product revealed a level of anger and rage I didn't know I had within me. The voice of a child was screaming to be heard. The other side was filled with hope in the Lord, forgiveness, grace, thankfulness, and a gentle peace I never knew I could have.

As part of the healing process to grieve the loss of childhood innocence, there are various programs to facilitate this difficult journey. Aware of the statistics on grief, some pastors are caring for their flocks in unique and innovative ways. Under the dynamic leadership of Pastor Marty Walker (www.alifethatthrives.com) at The Sanctuary Church in Santa Clarita, California, this generous church saw fit to invest in their congregants and paid for partial tuition for *The Grief Recovery Method Support Group.*[4] Our knowledgeable teacher, Gina Thompson, a Certified Grief Recovery Specialist, (www. scvgriefrecovery.com), guided us through the steps of grief recovery with her own honest, transparent, and vulnerable story. She modeled the necessary process so I could clearly examine the benefits, and sorrows, I derived from the experience with my particular loss. My experience with this process was profound. It changed my life dramatically. Later in this book, I will explain in greater detail how this class helped me to move forward.

Sadly, in our culture we are not taught how to process our grief or loss. Our fast-paced lives really don't allow for the time needed to grieve. Most corporate human resource policies only allow for three days of bereavement leave. And that's only if the loss is an immediate family member. Who of us can process the depth of grief in that short time period? Schools don't have any policy to allow for a student's absence in the event of the death of a family member. They may accept a note for a day or two away from school, but not much more than that. So we continue on and keep moving; working hard to compartmentalize the pain until it seeps out of our bodies and erupts in tears, anger, depression, disengagement, or rebellion. Or it can be turned inward and look like indifference, detachment, cutting, anorexia, bulimia, overeating, painkillers, illegal drugs, prescription drugs or any form of self-injury. I have lived through some of these experiences. I am still in the process of working through others.

When we face loss at a young age, we are encouraged to be strong, suck it up, and move on. We're told, "Don't let it get you down; there will be other people or things to replace your loss." Distraction is encouraged to avoid the pain and replace the sadness. This was true for me in becoming an overachieving maniac. I filled my life with distraction; work, activities, people, food. Especially in our technological culture, with electronic devices at our fingertips, we are heavily distracted from holding on to an uncomfortable feeling that brings us any level of conviction or discomfort. Rarely, will someone willingly seek the methodical process necessary to move past the hurt. Yet, somehow, the Lord provided a way for me to do so.

Whether we're facing the loss of a friendship, a major move from family or friends, a job change, the death of a parent, childhood innocence, the death of a child, our own physical health, or the loss of a marriage, it's a loss that requires time to grieve. If we want to gain some objectivity and appreciate the value of the loss, we must make the time to walk through it. If not, these losses accumulate and become so large that we lose perspective.

> IF WE WANT TO GAIN SOME OBJECTIVITY AND APPRECIATE THE VALUE OF THE LOSS, WE MUST MAKE THE TIME TO WALK THROUGH IT.

I gained great insight and healing as I worked through the sadness of my mother's passing and other losses I had long since buried. The various action steps of *Grief Recovery* allowed me to delve deeper into the anger, resentment, and blame that clouded my sorrow.

Most notably, many good memories were uncovered in the rubble of disappointment, shame, and anger regarding all the things I didn't receive. I needed time to reflect on the lifetime of value I had been given by acts of love as well as the disappointments I faced. Making the deliberate choice to focus on the losses for eight weeks, was a worthwhile investment in learning how to process a loss and experience the sense of freedom after the *Grief Support Group* was over.

Processing the death of my mom would prove to be timely and necessary as my father's health began to decline shortly after she died. Carrying all the emotions of her loss would have been staggering under the weight of my new role as caregiver for my father. Becoming his medical advocate, grocery shopper, and frequent meal provider threw me into a different relationship with him. It brought out feelings of great sadness and helplessness over his new status—widowhood after nearly seventy years of marriage.

My husband, Paul, and I decided to move from our comfortable surroundings to live closer to my father to care for his medical needs. All of this was largely consuming: packing up a home, looking for another home, and leaving the comfort of well-established relationships with our friends, church, doctors, dentists, hairstylist, etc. The emotional component of processing both the good, and the not so good, memories with my mother freed me up to now focus on my father's health issues and the details of our major move. This timely class helped me release the mental energy and the reoccurring tapes in my head that chose to recall only the hurt and disappointment.

The *Grief Support Group* showed me how to walk through the meaningful but forgotten experiences with my mom. They were buried under the debris of my own shame and anger. Although she was not physically affectionate, nor did she use encouraging words very often, I was able to recall all the times my mother had shown love to me in ways that she knew how. Acts of service were her comfort zone, and she demonstrated her love through creating a good meal, sewing a dress, keeping the house clean, attending an event I was involved in at school, working to provide things I needed, and caring for my sons. These were things I wanted to hold onto as part of my memories of her and not lose them among the piles of disappointment.

If I didn't have the opportunity to go through the *Grief Support Group* to process the depth of my grief, it would have been easier to stuff my feelings and not deal with them, only to face the fallout through grinding my teeth or overeating.

For me, not knowing how to clearly acknowledge many of my life's disappointments was like accumulating stones along the beach. As I walked the road of life, each unprocessed loss was another stone I held inside of me. They were collected in varying sizes and shapes, depending on the magnitude of the loss. Each occupied room within my soul. Having collected numerous stones over the years, both bulky and small, I was weighed down with a heaviness I couldn't explain. It was the kind of emotional pressure that makes you sigh from deep within. There was no room to breathe, listen to others, or be present in conversations. I was filled up with all these stones of sadness, disappointment, and regret. Working through my grief showed me how to take out each stone, examine it, acknowledge what happened, forgive those involved, own my part, if any, appreciate what I did have, and move forward. Now I am free to breathe deeply without the emotional heaviness, listen to others, and be emotionally and spiritually present to engage in another person's heartache.

Most recently, The Sanctuary Church paid for several church leaders to attend an intensive workshop on *Coaching for Christian Leaders*, by Keith Webb, (www.KeithWebb.com). I was fortunate to be included in this highly effective and pivotal workshop. I gained great value from learning how to allow the Holy Spirit to guide and direct our conversations by asking specific related questions. All too often, we halfway listen to someone's problem and then jump in to tell them how we would handle it. Or we tell them what they should do in that situation. If we rely on the Holy Spirit's guidance and ask the right questions, we can help someone find their *own* solution. This option usually creates a personal buy-in and motivates them to follow through because it's their *own* idea.

Since the *Coaching for Christian Leaders Workshop*, I've had the opportunity to use this skill set taught by Keith Webb. I have seen life changing results in speaking with people about the recurring problems they formerly could not get out of. When they are forced to ask themselves what the real problem is and how they think they can creatively change, new ideas emerge. They now can move in a direction towards a permanent solution.

I am truly grateful for the above-mentioned classes. Each one moved me closer to dealing with my pain, mistakes, internal sorrow, grief, and showed me ways to forgive and embrace the consistent, never-ending, love of my Heavenly Father.

10

REVELATION

Because of the Lord's great love we are not consumed,
for his compassions never fail. They are new
every morning; great is your faithfulness.

—Lamentations 3:22-23

There are so many examples of God's faithfulness for both my husband and me. God allowed us to be fully broken and completely dependent on His grace. It was through our pain and a desire to know this amazing love of the Father long before we met that reshaped and molded each of us into the persons we would attract and be attracted to. Individually, we sought a relationship with the Lord in His throne room and He invited us into His arms of peace and rest.

"Let the beloved of the Lord rest secure in him for he shields him all day long, and the one the Lord loves rests between his shoulders" (Deuteronomy 33:12).

Shortly after our marriage, we received the news that Oscar had a malignant brain tumor. I found out when Oscar called me from his hospital room on the day he was supposed to pick up our sons for his scheduled visitation. He had failed to share this information with me ahead of time so I could prepare the boys emotionally. Oscar had been diagnosed months before but had withheld the information. He said it wasn't important that I know his business, and he was just calling now because he wouldn't be there to pick up the boys. I didn't know when he would be able to see them.

Before he went into surgery, my sons and I were able to go to the hospital, tell him we forgave him, and release him to the Lord. We felt it was important for him to know he was forgiven, and he could go into this dangerous surgery without carrying any guilt. Within the next two years, Oscar would undergo another surgery for brain cancer and then a series of radiation treatments. During this time, God was doing a mighty work in both of our sons' hearts, and they had worked through much of the anger and hurt with their father.

Isaac, who had suffered much from his dad's erratic behavior, had a tender spot for his father and wanted to hold onto the good memories he cherished. He took his father groceries and to his doctor visits. He even cleaned up his house. Isaac would look for ways to love on his dad in the time they had together. God was healing their relationship through *His* forgiveness and love.

There was a short season when I could talk with Oscar about our sons. His admission to having an affair with the older woman who owned the ranch gave way to an acknowledgement for his behavior. He told me after I had taken him a home cooked meal following one of his surgeries, "Naomi, you didn't deserve my awful treatment toward you and the boys." He revealed he didn't know how to stop his dreadful behavior, as if it was something outside of him that was uncontrollable.

Although it didn't erase the horrible memories I still carried, I knew what had happened to me was unjust. The craziness of that surreal time now seemed to become real. He wasn't denying the hell he put us through. To my great pleasure, he was now genuinely interested in our sons' progress, and he actually listened while I shared my joy and concerns about their accomplishments and challenges. He was proud of them though he rarely told them that. Sometimes we would laugh at the funny things they would say or do. Finally, I was able to share with their direct bloodline the things my heart longed for. These two wonderful young men had been created in a time of love and hope in our relationship, and they were still the best part of our former marriage.

Even after an outpouring of love from his family, church, and our sons, Oscar's behavior began to regress. He called me around Christmas of 2009 to tell me he was planning to take me back to court to try to reduce his child support … again. Years before, he had failed to pay his court-ordered child support, and it was being automatically deducted from his paycheck. Due to his cancer diagnosis, his only check was his disability income. His voice was impatient and terse, without regard for the importance of the child support that helped care for his sons. I remember feeling like I was about to step on another roller coaster ride of high attorney's fees and disruptive court dates. The short-lived time of easy communication was now gone. Logic failed me in trying to explain the necessity of his small child support payments. Tears wet my face, and an anxious knot began to turn in my stomach.

Not wanting to reveal any of this to my boys, I snuck away to conceal my rising distrust of Oscar's new plans. There in the quiet of my bedroom, I turned to the Lord, knelt down, and prayed with my Bible open. I asked God to remove this mountain from me and the boys. The thought of Nathan having to endure four more years of court-ordered visitation with an angry, unpredictable, manipulative man was overwhelming.

"Truly I tell you, if anyone says to this mountain, "Go throw yourself into the sea, and does not doubt in their heart but believes that what they say will happen, it will be done for them" (Mark 11:23).

Two weeks later, Isaac called, crying on the phone, to tell me his dad had less than three weeks to live. Oscar died in January of 2010 from brain cancer. His request to his immediate family was to not have funeral services of any kind. My husband, Isaac, Nathan, and I wanted to honor the life that God had given their dad. We planned a simple memorial service so the boys could process their father's death and say some things at the service that were important to them. A week later, Isaac went into the Army. God was once again so faithful in allowing my son time to say goodbye to his dad and attend the memorial service before attending boot camp in February 2010.

The behavior Oscar exhibited during our marriage and most notably after we separated was not beneficial for a healthy relationship. He was a habitual liar who created his own world to support a false illusion of his life's accomplishments. He had no remorse for the pain he caused others and continued to go deeper into his fantasy life. Even after admitting his destructive choices, he continued to deceive, manipulate, and control others to satisfy his own selfish desires.

Much of what I and others observed appeared to be profound character issues. I want to be clear: I am not here to judge why Oscar made the decisions he did. My hope is to shed light on the characteristics of an abusive relationship. There remains the possibility that some, if not all, of Oscar's behavior could have been caused by his brain tumor which went undetected until it's later stages.

The joy and sadness for me in writing this is that I have seen great good that is reflected in the character of our sons. They are not perfect, but he would be very proud of them if he could see them today. They bring value to their relationships and consider others when making decisions.

You might be wondering what I have learned from this and how it has changed my perspective and relationship with the Lord.

I've learned that the Lord is forever faithful. He never left my side, despite how desperate I felt or how the circumstances looked. He fulfilled his promises of being, "**A Father to the Fatherless and a defender to the widows**" **(Psalm 68:5-6).**

God provided me with a loving God-honoring husband, a healthy marriage, and opportunities to learn and heal from my past hurts. He has brought new safe people into my life to listen to my story and help in the healing process. Rich opportunities have been presented to me that show me who I am in Christ and how I can serve others.

"I will repay you for the years the locust have eaten" (Joel 2:25).

Graciously, the Lord provided a steadfast family, pastors, and friends to love on us. Classes, counseling, words of encouragement, gifts, time with friends, and healing took place through these God-given, divine opportunities.

"He heals the brokenhearted and binds up their wounds" (Psalm 147:3).

He is our Provider. My sons and I were never without food, clothing, or shelter. Most importantly, the Lord provided relationships through loving family and friends, meaningful work, and school. He also provided counseling, for my younger son and me, through a wonderful woman, Carole Boersma, who helped us with her training in biblical counseling. He gave us hope.

"And my God will meet all your needs according to the riches of his glory in Christ Jesus" (Philippians 4:19).

Carole Boersma is a trained biblical counselor running *Restored Through Christ Ministries* (www.restoredthroughchrist-ministries.wordpress.com) in Saugus, California. For several years, she graciously worked with me as I waded through various issues of my past. The Lord gave her clarity to identify areas that needed to be addressed in my life. God knew I needed to clean house emotionally and spiritually before He could use me for greater things.

My husband, Paul, was also able to receive help from Carole. We were so blessed by her counsel that we have budgeted to support others who need counseling and restoration from their deep hurts. The Lord knows our wounds and had clearly told us that **"He heals the brokenhearted and binds up their wounds" (Psalm 147:3).** He also powerfully states, in **Isaiah 61:1, "The Spirit of the sovereign Lord is on me, because the Lord has anointed me to proclaim good news to the poor. He has sent me to bind up the brokenhearted, to proclaim freedom for the captives and release from darkness for the prisoners."**

"I will go before thee and make the crooked places straight: I will break in pieces the gates of brass and cut in sunder the bars of iron" (Isaiah 45:2, KJV).

This was especially evident in the courtroom. Here God was my advocate. He always went before me to make the crooked way straight. His voice was the one that brought justice to an unjust situation. He consistently provided despite the ways of man.

"Lord, you are a shield around me, my glory, the One who lifts my head high" (Psalm 3:3).

After hearing and reading about women who had been paralyzed or killed by being in terrifying situations like the ones shared in my story, I'm truly grateful that the Lord is my shield. He is the one who lifted my head in forgiveness to myself, and others, and removed the cloak of condemnation.

"He is my loving God and my fortress, my stronghold and my deliverer, my shield, in whom I take refuge, who subdues peoples under me" (Psalm 144:2).

After being padlocked out of our lovely home, the Lord provided a loving, safe, home for my sons and me. He went before us and even provided all of our furnishings, giving me back an exact replica of an entertainment center my sister had given me as a gift of love. The Lord comforted me with His arms of love through his provision.

"My people will live in peaceful dwelling places, in secure homes, in undisturbed places or rest" (Isaiah 32:18).

The fulfillment of this verse was evident in the lives of my sons and me as we were provided with a beautiful peaceful home. It was a safe place to welcome friends and family and give us the rest we needed to continue on.

"To bestow on them a crown of beauty instead of ashes, the oil of joy instead of mourning, and a garment of praise instead of a spirit of despair. They will be called oaks of righteousness. A planting of the Lord for the display of his splendor" (Isaiah 61:3).

I love this verse because I believe it describes my life. The Lord lifted me out of a pit of ashes and gave me great joy. He put on me a garment of praise for Him and His amazing goodness. He is planting seeds to encourage others who find themselves in despair through similar experiences or circumstances. He wants you to know there is great hope in His promises to us.

"Instead of your shame you will receive a double portion, and instead of disgrace you will rejoice in your inheritance. And so, you will inherit a double portion of your land, and everlasting joy will be yours" (Isaiah 61:7).

This is so specific to the mental script I struggled with most of my life. God was the only one who could remove that shame and guilt and replace it with honor because of the sacrifice of His Son, Jesus Christ. The hope of everlasting joy in the Lord is the greatest gift I could ever hope for. My Heavenly Father has been so faithful in restoring what was lost in a nearly fifteen-year marriage. He gave me back a double portion of what I lost and restored my honor and dignity.

"Train up a child in the way he should go: and when he is old, he will not depart from it" (Proverbs 22:6, KJV).

This scripture is one of the most significant to me as a tired, scared, and overwhelmed single mother. It is a clear reminder of God's abundant faithfulness to my inconsistent efforts to pour out His word into my sons' lives to engage them in activities that would build their character and to surround them with family and friends who would support and encourage them.

One of my greatest blessings is having my two sons. I am deeply proud of the men they have become and the choices they make every day to walk the straight and narrow road; to choose an honorable path and use the skills and resources God has given them.

I have been told I did a great job raising them. The truth is, they had an amazing Father. Their Heavenly Father was their guide, comforter, encourager, protector, and provided for them all along the way. He still is to this day.

I remember when Isaac needed to leave for boot camp weeks after his father's death. He was unable to process his grief among the insensitive, and sometimes brutal, structure of molding young men into soldiers. Hearing his tentative voice on the phone during his rare breaks, he shared how hard it was not to break down and cry in front of the others. No Sergeant would tolerate that kind of emotion. He pressed on. He continued his education and married a beautiful, godly, young woman. They worked together to finish their college degrees, obtain career jobs, and purchase a home. They have the most beautiful, little girl on the planet who brings tremendous joy to our family.

He is a caring son, loving husband, hard-working father, and a good friend to many. As a leader, he continues to serve our country and is pursuing an officer position with the Army.

Nathan's path has not been easy with all of the medical issues involving food allergies, asthma, and learning challenges. Due to his struggle to complete his high school curriculum, he chose not to continue on with traditional college classes. But, he has not given up and has found workable ways to educate himself and seek uncharted areas in which to excel. He is smart and insightful, and he thinks out of the box. I have no doubt that he will succeed in ways that far exceed his father and me.

I am proud of the courage and perseverance he has shown in carving out his own unique path in life. He is innovative and willing to take an unconventional route to get where he wants to go. He, like his brother, is handsome, personable, funny, and articulate. There is much more to come, but from what I've seen so far, I couldn't be more grateful for their individual choices.

There definitely were times, when I was going through these scary and demoralizing experiences, that I felt under attack—like a victim. I didn't understand why these terrible things were happened to me. After reading the Psalms, I realized God was allowing me to go through these life-shaping times, like King David had. He knew that God had *tried* him. **"See I have refined you, though not as silver; I have tested you in the furnace of affliction" (Isaiah 48:10).**

King David understood that the key was perseverance. He trusted God and believed He would bring him through his trials to a *place of abundance*. In my life, I have been blessed to experience the satisfaction and provision of God's blessings, materially and relationally. They spilled into every area of my life and the lives of my sons. God was my provider, my sustainer, my friend, my husband, and my protector through these challenging and uncertain times.

Often, my heart was encouraged reading the words of the Apostle Paul who teaches that, **"We also glory in our sufferings, because we know that suffering produces perseverance, perseverance character, and character hope" (Romans 5:3-4).** It is the act of persevering through trials that demonstrates our faith and allows God to complete His work in our lives. For me, it was only in retrospect that I have come to see the value of my suffering that draws me closer to God.

We've been given a freedom unknown to many. A freedom to walk confidently in the presence of the One who uniquely designed us in our mothers' wombs. Our spiritual fruit, gifts, talents, and attributes reveal our ability to walk in the freedom of the Lord.

"Now the Lord is the Spirit, and where the Spirit of the Lord is there is freedom" (2 Corinthians 3:17).

11

ENCOURAGEMENT
FOR EACH DAY

*It is not how much we have, but how much
we enjoy, that makes happiness.*

—Charles Spurgeon[1]

A few years ago, I heard of a book called *One Thousand Gifts*, by a talented and prolific author named Ann Voskamp (www.annvoskamp.com). She tells the story of the tragic loss of her baby sister as a young girl, the nervous breakdown of her mother, and her subsequent need to grow up quickly. Without time to process her losses, she suffered from depression and self-injury. As a dare, someone asked her to write out what she was thankful for each day. This simple act of daily journaling about her blessings revealed the goodness of God in both big and small ways.

I too, began a gratitude journal and numbered my entries to one thousand. Before long, I was looking for ways that the Lord would bless me each day. It was exciting, and at the same time tender, to see His loving hand on every area of my life.

This process was healing and affirming of His promises to me. Having a heart of gratitude toward the things I have learned on this journey has given me a clearer focus of how to serve others. It recalibrated my mind to a place of contentment for what I have, rather than what I lack.

> HAVING A HEART OF GRATITUDE TOWARD THE THINGS I HAVE LEARNED ON THIS JOURNEY HAS GIVEN ME A CLEARER FOCUS OF HOW TO SERVE OTHERS.

During the dark fearful times of my past, it seemed that my life was very small and closed off from hope. Fear had made my life small. Now I see through a lens of gratitude that my world has become larger and one with hopeful expectation. My Loving God is always ready and willing to provide good things to His children. He owns the cattle on a thousand hills and lacks absolutely nothing. (Psalm 50:10) Why should I doubt that He will provide the things I need or want to make my life full?

Seeing the value of my perspective and the mental trajectory it takes me to every day, I make a deliberate choice to look for the good in my life. This attitude causes me to want to share with others in ways that are simple and sincere about the hope we have in Christ. It is a practice I continue to make a part of my daily life.

"Never will I leave you; never will I forsake you" (Hebrews 13:5).

Reading my devotional by Sarah Young, *Jesus Calling*,[2] confirmed this act of deliberate gratitude. In it she writes:

> When you focus on what you don't have or on situations that displease you, your mind also becomes darkened. You take for granted life, salvation, sunshine, flowers, and countless other gifts from me. You look for what is wrong and refuse to enjoy life until that is 'fixed.'

When you approach me with thanksgiving, the light of my presence pours into you, transforming you through and through. Walk in the light with Me by practicing the discipline of Thanksgiving.

"I will offer You the sacrifice of thanksgiving and will call upon the name of the Lord" (Psalm 116:17, NKJV).

12

BEING THE HANDS AND FEET

You can't go back and change the beginning, but you can start where you are and change the ending.

—C. S. Lewis[1]

So, what does it look like to go from crisis to compassion? In my life, I see that if I call on the Lord and ask Him to show me how I can turn from my current crisis and help someone else, He is faithful to do that. Opportunities will become available and previously unknown doors will begin to open.

PROTECTING THOSE WHO CANNOT PROTECT THEMSELVES

This issue of childhood molestation runs deep within me. I have experienced firsthand the confusion, fear, and lack of trust it perpetuates. There is an indescribable terror that manipulates children to comply in this seduction of evil and a haunting distrust of their own body that responds physically to touch. Although we cannot erase the trauma and memories of this horrific experience, we can do something. Much support is needed for numerous organizations that work, usually on shoestring budgets, to provide life-changing services. Opportunities to give donations, volunteer, and work with and for organizations that devotedly serve the hurting are available to us everywhere.

World Health Organization Chart[2]

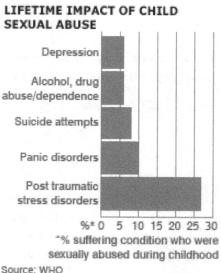

LIFETIME IMPACT OF CHILD SEXUAL ABUSE

%* 0 5 10 15 20 25 30

*% suffering condition who were sexually abused during childhood

Source: WHO

My husband and I support an effective organization called Zoe International, headquartered in Newhall, California. They address the physical, emotional, educational, and spiritual issues of children rescued from human trafficking in Thailand, Mexico, and Japan. Currently, they are preparing to build a home in Los Angeles, California to provide the same life-changing services to hurting and tormented children caught in the web of this evil, multi-layered, lucrative business of human trafficking.

We prayerfully and financially support a passionate and energetic young couple, named Cole and Abigail Jennerson (www.gozoe.org/jennersons), who work for Zoe in Thailand. These talented young people have sacrificed the comforts of carefree adult life in the United States to live in Thailand as Missionaries. They work together as husband and wife alongside several other missionaries from around the world serving these precious children. They have committed to learn the language, embrace the culture, adjust to the challenging climate, and subject themselves to the political dangers of living abroad. This is our way of supporting those who serve directly in the trenches of God's work.

Rape, abuse & Incest National Network[3]

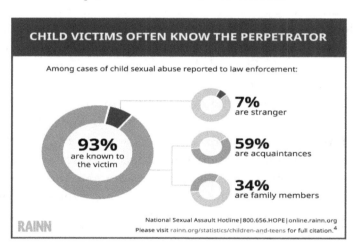

IMPACTING THOSE WHO LEARN DIFFERENTLY

Today, we hear about learning disabilities like Dyslexia, ADD/ADHD, and Autism. They are more talked about and researched than ever before. These disabilities adversely affect academic performance, self-esteem, self-worth, self-confidence, income, and the ability to provide for oneself. This powerful combination can cause tension within families that lead to marital division and sometimes divorce. The magnitude of their impact lasts a lifetime as these roadblocks to learning do not go away, and some are hereditary. They can negatively impact the dynamic within a family, classroom, and work environment.

In my experience as a Certified Professional Tutor working with children struggling with Dyslexia, Dysgraphia, and Attention Deficit Disorder, I have spoken with parents whose marriages were crumbling under the emotional, financial, and relational pressures of raising a child with a learning disability. Added to the family dynamics of marital pressures and addressing the needs of other children, they are faced with an institutionalized school system that teaches to the mainstream body of students. Most teachers are not taught in college how to identify children who are struggling with a learning disability, and the problem can go undiagnosed for years. Some of these hard-working teachers must pay out of their own resources and take classes on their own time to investigate ways of teaching these forgotten students.

Typically, a child must be two years or more behind their grade level in order to qualify for any Special Education services provided by the school district. This dramatic delay causes additional trauma and heartache well beyond the classroom.

Very few school districts will prioritize funds to provide training to teachers on the current research for learning disabilities. These determined teachers are often at a loss to effectively identify and teach children who learn differently. Insufficient school funding and growing classroom size contribute to the ever-demanding jobs placed on exhausted and poorly-paid teachers. This only causes more issues to arise with the child as they navigate their way through the demoralizing rigors of elementary, middle, and high school education. By the time many in this vast population of teetering children enter high school, they are angry, rebellious, and have adopted a negative script of self-talk, filled with, "I can't do it, so why try." I have witnessed this all too often with my students and in my own life.

Overwhelmed parents are also unaware of why things are so difficult for their child. First, if they choose to invest the time, they must become self-educated on the symptoms and tests available to accurately diagnose their child. Then they must become their child's advocate throughout the years of maneuvering through the educational labyrinth. This is their hope; that someday they can hand the baton over to the now young adult who must step into a larger arena of life and begin the process of survival.

In addition to their learning battles, years of struggling, bullying by other students, and feeling different without understanding why, much bigger problems have risen. These include, acquiring and maintaining a job, communicating in relationships, understanding how to maneuver through the bureaucratic maze of insurance companies, unemployment, and Social Security benefits. Any one of these can be daunting. These invisible disabilities exist for many who look perfectly capable of handling life's varied challenges. It's the internal disconnect with themselves, their families, and the world around them that makes having a learning disability all the more confusing. Many often lose hope and give up, turning to other things.

So many of these individuals with learning challenges have wonderful talents in the arts. All too often, these gifts lie dormant under the constant barrage of homework assignments, and behavior issues, that have developed from the confusion of this difference among their peers. I have seen my students light up at the chance to work with their hands instead of with pen and paper. Artistic ideas border their class notes with pictures of superheroes or adventures that go unfulfilled in their minds.

I HAVE SEEN MY
STUDENTS LIGHT UP
AT THE CHANCE TO
WORK WITH THEIR
HANDS INSTEAD OF
WITH PEN AND PAPER.

I used to make jewelry and had an abundance of supplies at one end of my office. One day, I decided to encourage a student who was having difficulty concentrating on his tutoring assignment. So I told him if he could try his best throughout our tutoring time I would reserve the last ten minutes of our session for him to create whatever he wanted to out of my jewelry supplies. His eyes glazed over as he looked at the organic stones, leather, wire, and Swarovski crystals. "You mean, you'll let me use all of your cool stuff?" I told him he could use any of my supplies he needed to create what he wanted.

Well this proved to be an amazing new direction for him. From then on, he continued to put forth his best effort at the beginning of our sessions knowing that he would be able to do something creative during his last ten minutes. He designed a beautiful innovative necklace for his mother, filled with mixed media metals and choice stones of various colors. He worked on it steadily until Christmas so he could provide this gift for her, which was made from a part of himself that had been undiscovered for years. To him, it was a way of telling his mother how thankful he was for her persistence to find him help.

On Christmas morning, I received a telephone call. On the other end of the phone was a voice that sounded shaky and filled with tears. I couldn't understand who it was at first, and then she identified herself as my student's mother. This grateful mom told me that she had received the most beautiful gift from her son—a gift that she would cherish forever. She, ironically, was a talented artist but never knew her son held this hidden gem within himself along with a desire to design and create. A few years later, while taking classes at a local community college, he created a wonderful skyline sculpture out of polyvinyl chloride (PVC) pipes and brought it over to my home to show me.

One by one, I have seen students come to my office, and after their tutoring sessions, they'd create some of the most magnificent pieces of artwork I've ever seen. Each one was eager to develop a side of themselves that had gone untapped. When the focus was off of their deficit, they were able to soar. What a lesson this was for me to see the power of encouragement.

So what are some ways you can help those who struggle? There are volunteer opportunities at elementary, junior high, and high schools where you live. Teachers are given the difficult task of teaching twenty or more children at a time, all with different learning capabilities. Most schools are equipped with funding for Special Education or Resource classes to give a child some extra instruction outside the main classroom. I'm sure the teachers, parents, and students would welcome a willing and caring assistant or volunteer to come alongside them in the meaningful work of teaching the next generation how to become employable citizens.

Being a Certified Professional Tutor is a rewarding field of work. You can earn a respectable salary, manage your own schedule, and work with students and parents with current, effective, research tools available for various learning challenges. There are many certification programs available to train tutors. For reading, spelling, and comprehension, I recommend an Orton Gillingham based program. It is research-based using sequential and systematic methods that are highly effective. There are too few trained tutors in this field to address the growing numbers of struggling children and families needing specific support. The need, and opportunities, to impact lives with hopeful possibilities are tremendous.

Key facts about Dyslexia Chart [4]

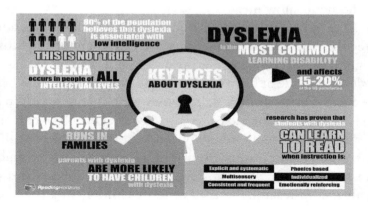

The National Center for Educational Statistics says the number of public school students receiving Special Education services in 2015-2016 reached 6.7 million. That is about 13 percent of all public-school students. Within those receiving Special Education services, 34 percent had a specific learning disability. Studies show those with learning disabilities earn less income than those without. According to an article in the *Guardian News* on April 13, 2011 by Janet Snell, she wrote that only 6.4 percent of people with learning disabilities are in paid employment. That is a sad statistic, reflecting human potential that is left behind.

Obesity is at a higher rate for those with learning disabilities as opposed to mainstream students. Divorce rates also rank higher among this population, with some quoting as high as 80 percent for those couples with a special needs child. There are so many good reasons to reach out to students, teachers, parents, and siblings who are impacted by those with learning challenges.

Dyslexia and Reading Proficiency[5]

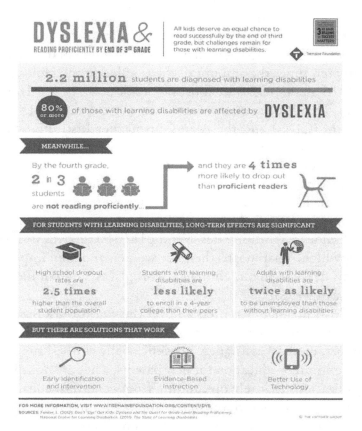

Giving is the highest expression of potency. In the very act of giving, I experience my strength, my wealth, and my power. This experience of heightened vitality and potency fills me with joy. I experience myself as overflowing, spending, and alive; hence as joyous. Giving is more joyous than receiving, not because it is a deprivation, but because in the act of giving lies the expression of my aliveness. —Erich Fromm

ADDRESSING THE IMPACT OF ABORTION

This issue of abortion can be overwhelming. Nearly 60 million abortions have taken place since the infamous court decision of *Roe v. Wade* legalized abortion in the United States. That's nearly ten times the amount of those killed in the Holocaust. In 2016 alone, 893,000 abortions took place in the United States. This 2008 statistic comes from the Centers for Disease Control (CDC) and the Alan Guttmacher Institute, which serves as the research arm for Planned Parenthood, the largest abortion provider in the United States (www.guttmacher.org/pubs/fb_induced_abortion.html#5). Based on the 2008 Abortion Patient Survey, one in three women will have an abortion by age 45. Although, this is subject to change, with the decline in abortion rates over the last 10 years, it's still startlingly high. That means there are women and men impacted by this decision in our churches, workplaces, and families. So what can we do?

Crisis pregnancy centers all over the world work tirelessly to provide free pregnancy tests, health education, emotional support, medical assistance, life skills, baby clothes, supplies, and continuing education for new parents. They are non-profit organizations that rely on funding from generous, consistent donors to keep their doors open. Volunteer opportunities are in abundance and often may lead to a paid position for these worthy organizations. If your forte is fund-raising, you may want to offer your experience or creativity to increase finances and keep the pregnancy center running in your area. Case managers, receptionist, nurses, bookkeepers, and custodians are welcomed to perform various duties as volunteers or paid personnel.

Unfortunately, of the approximately 3,000 crisis pregnancy centers in the U.S., few have the resources and staff available to provide post-abortion counseling classes to the vast numbers of women and men negatively impacted by this fatal decision. Churches often lack the staff to offer these healing resources and some pastors avoid delving into this topic from the pulpit. Additionally, it is a political hot potato for elections, polarizing people at both ends of the opinion poll. Even fewer individuals will voluntarily offer this information in public, due to the stigma of shame or fear of rejection. Many have not come to terms with the barbaric procedures involved in their own abortion and the recent revelation of some abortion centers selling baby body parts for profit.

Several post-abortive women are being empowered to share their stories from a culture that supports a woman's right to choose but fails to give adequate information on the ramifications of that *choice*. Here are some honest and raw quotes from women who have been betrayed by that *choice* and worked in the abortion industry. Lori Nerad[6], a former National President of Women Exploited by Abortion says:

> We as a society are constantly bombarded with the pro-choice rhetoric that abortion is sometimes necessary. We also hear the words of post-abortive women like Celine Richards, Chief Executive Officer of Planned Parenthood, who will say that their abortions were the right thing to do. But whether they are stuffing down their emotions or just plain lying, abortion is never a happy ending.
>
> It kills a child and leaves a Mother to live the rest of her life with the knowledge that she took her child's life. Nothing brings that pain to light better than the words directly from the mouths of everyday post-abortive Mothers who are ignored by the major media outlets. Unlike Richards, these women have nothing to gain from sharing their stories. They only hope to help other Mothers choose life.

Another forthright proclamation to this culturally acceptable *quick procedure* is honestly and painfully shared by former abortion worker, Jewels Green[7]:

After an abortion, the instrument tray was passed through the window in the wall into the auto clave room. The other thing that passed through was the *Jar*. It held the precious contents that just moments before had comfortably resided inside the mother's womb.

It looked like an oversized glass pickle jar. It was emptied next to me on the counter top: teeny tiny hands and feet and arms and legs and a rib cage and a spine and a hollow, flattened, misshapen, torn head.

I saw it all.
I smelled it all.
Every time. Up to 30 times a day, four days a week …

I started having nightmares, haunted by tiny, limbless phantom babies. I was floating down a narrow stream with miniature body parts strewn on either shore—and then I'd begin to sink. I'd flail and gasp and go under.

There are, however, some great organizations who provide pivotal support to the emotionally, mentally, and spiritually scarred adults who are part of this large horrifying statistic. They are reaching out to provide biblical support and healing through our Lord Jesus Christ. One such organization is Ramah International.

The solution Ramah International is providing our world is based on **Jeremiah 31:16: "This is what the Lord says, Restrain your voice from weeping and your eyes from tears. For your work will be rewarded. Your children will return from the land of the enemy."**

Ramah International's purpose is to bring individuals struggling with post-abortion syndrome to healing, that they might cease their mourning through the grieving of their children's deaths and be released from their grief to live a normal life. It is heartbreaking work to touch this pain yet helping them to acknowledge the loss of their children is the first step to post-abortion syndrome healing. In time, their *work* will be rewarded.

When a person suffering from post-abortion syndrome names their child, the child becomes a permanent part of their parents' hearts. In my own experience while working at the SCVPC, I saw women healed from the emotional pain after naming their child lost through an abortion. It brought a clarifying reality to the life that was lost. I too, experienced this profound closure in naming my child.

The Result of Ramah International's work is supported by **Jeremiah 31:17a: "So there is hope for your future, declares the Lord."**

What is the hope of someone suffering post-abortion syndrome? For many, it is stopping abortion from hurting other lives. This ministry believes that through the healed voices of the post-abortive who attest to the devastation abortion caused them, the abortion figures will be reduced. Post-abortive individuals are strong voices who can attest to the fact that abortion is a horrible choice—not only for the mother but also for the child. They are excellent in ministering to the abortion-minded individual.

Sydna Masse, founder of Ramah International, Inc., is the compassionate author of the powerful book, *Her Choice to Heal: Finding Spiritual and Emotional Peace After Abortion*, and the companion Recovery Guide,[8] that takes the reader through the critical steps of grief (www.HerChoicetoHeal.com). This book is laced with relevant scripture as it addresses the rarely discussed symptoms of post-abortion syndrome. Written with transparency and honesty, like one who has walked through the throes of pain from this disastrous decision, these are great resources for pregnancy centers, churches, or support groups for the post-abortive who are suffering.

U.S. Women Who Have Abortions[9]

As a way of being the hands and feet of Christ, you may consider donating these books and study guides to your local pregnancy center, church, or support group for women struggling with post-abortion. There are also some valuable healing books for men on this subject. One I recommend is *Healing the Father's heart: A Post-Abortion Bible Study for Men* authored by Linda Cochrane and Kathy Jones. This unique book provides practical information to guide men through the stages of post-abortion syndrome and helps them to find hope and comfort through Jesus Christ.

Being part of a supportive community while processing your grief from an abortion is vital. As mentioned earlier, this had a profound effect on my healing process. I was infused with hope from real people. In addition to pregnancy centers and churches, there are organizations, like *Deeper Still* (www.godeeperstill.org), that provide weekend healing retreats for men and women all over the United States. Additionally, they provide training seminars and materials. Look for a Chapter in your area to receive the life-changing benefits and much-needed healing to free your abortion-wounded heart.

Walking through the grief of an abortion is critical for processing the deeply held pain, regret, and self-punishing behaviors that keep us trapped in the enemy's camp. One prolific author, who has walked the path of grief from the loss of her husband to Lou Gehrig's Disease (ALS), is Susan VandePol. She beautifully describes the process of dealing with her grief as she runs into the arms of Jesus and dearly holds onto His Word for strength, courage, and daily sustenance. In her debut book, *Life after breath,*[10] (www.mattersoflifeand-breath.com), she describes grief as follows:

> God is immeasurably entrenched in your grief, and His compassion never ceases or fails to do what it set out to accomplish (Lamentations 3:32-33). The compassion of God means he is co-passionate with you. He feels with you and co-suffers with you --- literally. It was His passion that brought Him to earth and led Him to the cross, and it is His passion that left His Spirit here to keep you breathing. It heals you, sustains you, restores you, and anoints you for the task at hand.

> It will take some time ... probably a long time; don't let anyone kid you or dismiss the agony or longevity of grief because where the Spirit of the Lord is—the source of your breath—there is freedom, and that means freedom to grieve. The loss is worthy of the effort and the honor.

Yes, Susan is right. It does take time, and your loss is worthy of every moment it takes to process it. Be kind to yourself and allow the time and space to grieve your loss. No one can put a time limit on your grief and how it should look. Filtering through our unmet expectations, hopes, and disappointments looks different for each one of us. You and the life of your loved one are worth the time this transition requires.

Unfortunately, many of us opt for the quick fix. Rarely are we willing to enter the long road to healing. But here is where we see God's footsteps right next to our own. He only gives us enough for each day. There is no way to escape the healing process if we want to be free from the shackles of pain and disappointment. No shortcuts. It's short pain now, as we enter in and embrace it, or long-term pain as we try to avoid the reminders of our heartache. This process has made, and is making, a profound difference in my own life as I have attested to.

Be aware there are triggers everywhere. Especially when we hear about the issue of abortion in the news, politics, Right to Life Sunday, or are sitting at a baby shower with friends and family who don't know about our abortion. A deliberate decision to cross the river of pain and embrace God's awaiting arms shows respect for yourself. Cleaning house on the pain that keeps you from moving forward in relationships, with honesty and transparency, is worth the temporary discomfort of facing your heartache.

REACHING OUT TO SINGLE PARENT FAMILIES

According to single parent statistics and based on the U.S. Census Bureau in December 2011, there were about 13.7 million single-parent families in the U.S. today raising 22 million children. That's a lot of opportunity to reach out to a tired mother or father doing the job of two parents. There are so many organizations designed to support the children and parents of these families, including Big Brothers/Big Sisters, Boys and Girls Clubs, Single Parent Ministries at churches, AWANA for Kids, Adopt-a-Family programs for holiday events, etc.

Any way you choose to turn your crisis or the crisis of someone else into compassion speaks volumes about the love of Christ within you. God never wastes anything and will use the smallest act of kindness for His Glory. He will magnify your monetary donations, your time, and words of encouragement to bless many people. Reaching out and being the hands and feet of Christ will always bring you joy because the joy is always in the giving.

> "FROM WHAT WE GET, WE CAN MAKE A LIVING; WHAT WE GIVE, HOWEVER, MAKES A LIFE" (ARTHUR ASHE).[11]

The time to dare to make a positive difference in the life of another is now. There will always be something else to work on, some distraction that changes your focus. You are needed. Your skills, talents, attitude, ideas, finances, and your love are valuable. Sometimes we just need to step out and try. Most would rather sit back and complain, letting someone else fix the problems we face in society. Life is messy, but it is most fulfilling when we participate in it.

Stepping out and trying is best articulated in one of my favorite speeches from President Theodore Roosevelt. He gave a compelling speech called, *Citizenship in a Republic.*[12] It has often been referred to as "The Man in the Arena," and he delivered it at the Sorbonne in Paris, France on April 23, 1910. Here is the passage that made this speech famous:

> It is not the critic who counts; not the man who points out how the strong man stumbles, or where the doer of deeds could have done them better.

> The credit belongs to the man who is actually in the arena, whose face is marred by dust and sweat and blood; who strives valiantly; who errs, who comes short again and again,

> Because there is no effort without error and shortcoming; but who does actually strive to do the deeds; who knows

great enthusiasms, the great devotions; who spends himself in a worthy cause;

Who at the best knows in the end the triumph of high achievement, and who at the worst, if he fails, at least fails while daring greatly...

If we wait until everything is perfect before we walk into the arena of life, we shortchange ourselves and others who want to jump in the ring with us and dare to make a difference. Opportunities and relationships are waiting to be taken. If we prolong getting involved, we forfeit making a contribution while we had the chance. The time, connection with others, and use of our gifts cannot be recovered.

> IF WE WAIT UNTIL EVERYTHING IS PERFECT BEFORE WE WALK INTO THE ARENA OF LIFE, WE SHORTCHANGE OURSELVES AND OTHERS WHO WANT TO JUMP IN THE RING WITH US AND DARE TO MAKE A DIFFERENCE.

At the end of our days, we want to look back without regrets. The visual that comes to my mind is the Dead Sea. I don't want to be like this hypersaline lake in the Middle East that receives runoff water but gives out nothing. It is a harsh place that supports no life; no fish or aquatic plants can survive there. Basically, it continually receives but never gives out. What a stark picture of a life that doesn't pour out to the needs around us. I seriously doubt if anyone can live a fulfilled life by holding on to all the good things that come their way and never give away anything. The truly fulfilled life is experienced when we live intentionally with joy-filled giving.

Mother Teresa[13] wisely explains to us:

At the end of life, we will not be judged by how many diplomas we have received, how much money we have made, how many great things we have done. We will be judged by 'I was hungry and you gave me to eat, I was naked and you clothed me, I was homeless and you took me in.' Hungry not only for bread—but hungry for love. Naked not only for clothing—but naked for human dignity and respect. Homeless not only for want of a room of bricks—but homeless because of rejection.

"It is more blessed to give than receive" (Acts 20:35).

"Give, and it will be given to you. Good measure, pressed down, shaken together, running over, will be put into your lap. For with the measure you use it will be measured back to you" (Luke 6:38).

13

EYES WIDE OPEN

You may choose to look the other way, but you can never say again that you did not know.

—William Wilberforce[1]

Now that you've read Naomi Parker's vulnerable story of perseverance in the face of staggering circumstances and have rejoiced in the mighty, restorative, hand of God, what does this look like in your own life? Are you willing to trust God in those scary and regretful places? Will you risk being transparent with someone else and tell your own story? Will you let God do a mighty work in your life and the lives of those around you?

Honestly life is messy and wading through the issues of life is never easy. I willingly admit the only relationship that has brought me true peace is a relationship with Jesus Christ.

I hope you are already aware, but if you are not, there is a wonderful, kind, generous, and forgiving God who loves you so much that He sent His only son to die on a cross in your place, for your sins. He desires an honest relationship with you as His child but not in the formality of religion. He stands at the door and knocks. If you want to walk through this life intimately with your Maker, then stop now and bow your head in reverence to Him. Speak to Him in your own words and acknowledge that He is God. Tell Him you believe that He sent His only Son to take your place on the cross so that after you leave this earth, you can enjoy eternal life with Him in Heaven. Tell Him you believe His Son, Jesus Christ, rose from the grave three days after he was buried. Ask Him to forgive your sins, mistakes, and wrong decisions. Tell him you desire to know more about Him and will seek Him with all your heart, soul, mind, and strength. Ask Him to come into your life and occupy every corner of your being. Amen!

After asking the Lord into my life I have had no regrets. Things didn't change overnight, but slowly a transformation has taken place. Fear has been replaced with trust and confusion with clarity. Knowing the truth, I now live in freedom.

> I HOPE YOU ARE ALREADY AWARE, BUT IF YOU ARE NOT, THERE IS A WONDERFUL, KIND, GENEROUS, AND FORGIVING GOD WHO LOVES YOU SO MUCH THAT HE SENT HIS ONLY SON TO DIE ON A CROSS IN YOUR PLACE, FOR YOUR SINS.

If you did that, welcome to the family of God! You can learn more about God and His Son, Jesus, by reading the Book of John in the Holy Bible. Then, read the Psalms and Proverbs about the promises He offers and the clear guidelines He gives us to live this life fully. You could also start by reading the Book of Genesis, in the beginning of the Bible, to give you a history of how God created the earth and everything in it. Find a Bible teaching church and most of all, pray (talk to God) every day, and ask Him for direction. He will give you the wisdom and guidance needed to live your life as His child.

We know that we have an advocate by our side, but please be very clear there is a real and vicious enemy who exists to annihilate us. His very purpose is to kill, steal, and destroy you (John 10:10). He is cunning, coy, and extremely patient. He is the angel of darkness, but he also disguises himself as the angel of light (2 Corinthians 11:14), the master of deception (Daniel 8:23), and the father of lies (John 8:44). The enemy is also known as the prince of darkness, orchestrator of seduction, director of destruction, navigator of negativity, author of confusion, delegator of shame, master of manipulation, magnifier of despair, enforcer of mayhem, and the generator of fear. He rejoices in your punishment; he is never for you and will use you for his own gain. He will steal your joy, magnify your heartache, and seduce you into thinking you are doing well. He torments us all with fear and death. He is void of all hope. He is the king of hell and will do everything in his power to lure you into his kingdom so you can join him in his eternal destruction. He carefully and systematically distracts you from your true purpose—to honor and glorify the Lord God Almighty.

> WE KNOW THAT WE HAVE AN ADVOCATE BY OUR SIDE, BUT PLEASE BE VERY CLEAR THERE IS A REAL AND VICIOUS ENEMY WHO EXISTS TO ANNIHILATE US.

This enemy is a wolf in sheep's clothing who parades as a truth bearer but mixes it with lies. He will tell you a thousand truths, just to tell you one lie. He is always trying to trip you up and lead you astray. Be careful not to be fearful or anxious because he is a defeated foe, and his time is short.

What an enormous ongoing effort this is by this evil master and his flock of demons. You have something he wants: the ability to honor and serve the One who created you and do good works on His behalf. With Christ in you, you reflect the hope of His glory. As you step out into the light of Jesus Christ and serve others, be prepared for a battle. Put on your spiritual armor and be the hands and feet of Jesus Christ. God has equipped you for such a time as this to do His work, and He *will* protect you (Esther 4:14).

Ephesians 6:10-18 states:

> Be strong in the Lord and in His mighty power. Put on the full armor of God so that you can take your stand against the devil's schemes. For our struggle is not against flesh and blood, but against the rulers, against the authorities, against the powers of this dark world and against the spiritual forces of evil in the heavenly realms. Therefore put on the full armor of God so that when the day of evil comes, you may be able to stand your ground, and after you have done everything to stand. Stand firm then with the belt of truth buckled around your waist, with the breastplate of righteousness in place, and with your feet fitted with the readiness that comes from the gospel of peace. In addition to all this, take up the shield of faith, which you can extinguish all the flaming arrows of the evil one. Take the helmet of salvation and the sword of the Spirit, which is the word of God.

Being prepared for daily battle is critical to thrive as an effective believer. No true soldier has ever gone on a battlefield to face his enemy without adequately putting on protective gear and spending time in training with weapons that will defeat his enemy. If we do not enter the battle prepared, we do so at our own peril.

God's Word tells us in **1 Peter 5:6-9, "Be self-controlled and alert. Your enemy, the devil, prowls around like a roaring lion looking for someone to devour."**

The Apostle Peter, who loved Jesus deeply and told Him he would never betray Him, was nearly taken out by Satan. Peter dramatically told Christ he would never deny Him. And yet, because of his accusers, he was so overcome with fear about his association with Jesus that he quickly denied any knowledge of Christ. Peter was consumed by the fear of death that could come from admitting he knew Christ. As a result, he denied Him three times despite his emotional vow to never disown his Master. The flesh and the devil are impossible to fight without the Word of God. Without the armor of God and knowledge of His Word we are subject to doubt, distraction, defeat, and discouragement. We ask ourselves the same question Eve wrestled with in the garden: Did God really mean this? Is this problem, pain, or punishment really his will for me? Doesn't God want me to be happy? Without spending time reading His powerful Word to us in the Bible, and taking time to hear His voice, we cannot know His will and direction for our lives.

Even Jesus, after being baptized by His cousin, John the Baptist, and confirmed by the Holy Spirit, was led into the wilderness for forty days to be tempted by Satan. How did He endure this torment? He was filled up with the Holy Spirit. So, if Jesus, who is the Son of God, needed to maintain intimate relational communication with His Father to fulfill His destiny, wouldn't we need to do the same? Especially, because we have so many more distractions in this modern age than He did.

"And Jesus returned in the power of the Spirit to Galilee, and a report about Him went out throughout all the surrounding country. And He taught in their synagogues, being glorified by all" (Luke 4:14).

Then Jesus went into Nazareth where he grew up, and he went into a synagogue on the Sabbath. He went to Nazareth to speak the truth about who He is and His purpose for coming. There He stood and read from the scroll of the prophet, Isaiah, that was given to Him. After unrolling the scroll, He found the place (Luke 4:18-19) where it was written:

> The Spirit of the Lord is upon me, because He has anointed me to proclaim good news to the poor. He has sent me to proclaim liberty to the captives and recovering of sight

to the blind, to set at liberty those who are oppressed, to proclaim the year of the Lord's favor.

So, brothers and sisters in Christ, victory is in sight. The life-changing story of Christ has been told. His truth has been spoken, and His light has been brought to the dark places. If Jesus was assaulted by the enemy, are we any different? He was able to combat the slippery accusations of the enemy, because Jesus spent time with His Father and the Word His Father instilled in Him. Fully aware of the magnitude of the oppression His disciples would experience after His ascension, Jesus told the twelve He would be leaving them with His powerful Holy Spirit. He desired for them—and us—to have the sweet intimacy of an ever-present counselor, comforter, and friend. The Holy Spirit is the One who speaks truth into our lives like no other. He's gentle, kind, loving and convicting. He enables us to live the life we are called to.

The disciples who followed Jesus did not escape the treacherous ways of the enemy either. They were ridiculed, chased, beaten, stoned, flogged, shipwrecked, put in prison, hung upside down, and beheaded for their faith in Christ. Placed there for a purpose, these men and women chose to follow, with various depths of understanding, the selfless lessons taught by Christ. They clung to His promises and were encouraged, until their last breath, through the community of believers.

During my darkest days, it was a community of loving believers that pulled me out of the shadow of despair. Without their faith, hope, and love for a better future, I don't know how I would have been able to push through the darkness. They were a living example of the hands and feet of Christ.

What are we to do? As mentioned above, we are to stand strong in the power of *His* might, put on the full armor of God, and not be intimidated by the devil's schemes. We pray in the Spirit on all occasions. We are to pray for each other both near and far. We are to rest in the gift of His peace for us and *not fear*. The words *fear not* actually appear more than 80 times in the Bible. The Lord knows the enemy will use this tactic to paralyze us, minimize our hope in Christ, and erase any victory for the Kingdom of God.

"So, do not fear, for I am with you; do not be dismayed, for I am your God. I will strengthen you and help you; I will uphold you with my righteous right hand" (Isaiah 35:4).

"Have I not commanded you? Be strong and courageous. Do not be afraid; do not be discouraged, for the LORD your God will be with you wherever you go" (Joshua 1:9).

Rest in the Power of the One who goes before you to level the mountains (Isaiah 45:2) and makes your way straight. He is riding at the helm in this epic spiritual battle. He is the Lord of the armies of heaven (Revelation 19:14). Our God is mighty, powerful, and strong (Genesis 1:1). He is the only One who has created something from nothing. Only He can declare what will happen before it occurs (Isaiah 42:9). He supplies us with strength and equips us for battle. As my Shepherd, He not only feeds my soul but protects me as well (Psalm 23). Only He has an endless supply to meet our every need (Ephesians 3:20). He is my Banner, my Deliverer, and He goes before me in battle. The battle is His (1 Samuel 17:47). Nothing is too difficult for Him (Jeremiah 32:17).

The battle is truly the Lord's, but in His wisdom, He allows us to fight alongside Him through the weapon of prayer. He is the Anchor of our souls (Hebrews 6:19), the Captain of the armies of heaven (Joshua 5:14), the Bright and Morning Star (Revelation 22:16), the Prince of Peace (Isaiah 9:6). We are more than conquerors through Him who loves us (Romans 8:37), overcomers in this life (1 John 5:4), and we have been made victorious through the blood of Jesus Christ (Revelation 12:11). What wonderful promises we stand on, given to us by the God of Hope (Romans 15:13).

"For I am convinced that neither death nor life, neither angels nor demons, neither the present nor the future, nor any powers, neither height nor depth, nor anything else in all creation, will be able to separate us from the love of God that is in Christ Jesus our Lord" (Romans 8:38-39).

Jesus leaves us with two of the greatest commandments: **"Love the Lord your God with all your heart and with all your soul, and with all your strength, and with all your mind; and love your neighbor as yourself"** (Luke 10:27). This is especially true in the household of God. We are not alone in this life. Inwardly, we have God's Holy Spirit to comfort and guide us. Outwardly, we have other believers with whom to walk through this life. This is not an optional statement—it is a command. It's not just me and God but a family of believers (1 John 4:20). God has provided for our spiritual, emotional, physical, and relational needs.

"Be strong and courageous. Do not fear or be in dread of them, for it is the Lord your God who goes with you. He will not leave you or forsake you" (Deuteronomy 31:6, ESV).

"Say to those with fearful hearts, 'Be strong, do not fear; your God will come, he will come with vengeance; with divine retribution. He will come to save you'" (Isaiah 35:4).

We have been given a powerful gift that is exclusive to believers: the peace of God. He knew this would be needed to calm our anxious hearts and minds. He has equipped us, not only with His impenetrable armor and comforting Word, but also His unique and precious gift of peace. There is no material item, or earthly comfort, that can compare with God's loving bestowal of His calming presence of peace.

Counter-intuitive to the world we live in—a world that defaults to worry, stress and fear—we can have an uncommon peace. When we hear an alarming diagnosis, confront an unfaithful spouse, struggle with a rebellious child, or face the finality of the death of a loved one, it's in those paralyzing times that we can encounter God's peace. Ultimately by leaving our worries at His feet, we can find true rest in Christ. This is the peace of the Lord that transcends all understanding.

COUNTER-INTUITIVE TO THE WORLD WE LIVE IN—A WORLD THAT DEFAULTS TO WORRY, STRESS AND FEAR—WE CAN HAVE AN UNCOMMON PEACE.

"Peace I leave with you; my peace I give to you. Not as the world gives do I give to you. Let not your hearts be troubled, neither let them be afraid" (John 14:27, ESV).

These powerful promises for believers are the lifeblood of Christian living. We trust our God and acknowledge His goodness. Allowing Him and His Word into the process of our daily struggles and victories, He gladly shows up to walk this journey with us. Jesus tells us clearly that, **He will never leave us or forsake us (Hebrews 13:5): "I am with you always, even to the end of the age" (Matthew 28:20).**

Today, let me encourage you to commit all your circumstances to God. Allow his peace to transcend your concerns. Focus on His Word and His precious promises specifically for you. He always has more for us than our present conditions may dictate. If you experience difficulties, stay faithful. Continue to trust in Him. He is faithful to open the doors we need to walk through and close those that are not to our benefit.

"You have made known to me the path of life; you will fill me with joy in your presence, with eternal pleasures at your right hand" (Psalm 16:11).

I'd like to leave you with the words of my wonderful husband, Paul, who continues to tell me, "God will take a lifetime to use you for a short-time." Nothing is ever wasted.

"But you are a chosen generation, a royal priesthood, a holy nation, His own special people, that you may proclaim the praises of Him who called you out of darkness into His marvelous light" (1 Peter 2:9, NKJV).

"Let us consider how to spur one another on to love and good deeds. Let us not give up meeting together as some are in the habit of doing but let us encourage one another — and all the more as you see the Day approaching" (Hebrews 10: 24-25).

AFTERWORD

This story has been rewritten in my head for years, wondering if it would ever be safe to share my deep shame without the judgement of others. Slowly, these stories have seeped out of my pores and flowed out through intimate conversations. Carefully, watching the reactions of others—sadness, shock, anger or triggers from past memories—has opened the gate to take these steps in sharing this overwhelming story.

Several decades later, when the raging waters seized to overtake me, I decided to step into the deep and become a truth teller. First a toe, then a foot, now waist high, I'm getting comfortable in the water and starting to splash around in its cleansing joy.

My hope in writing this journey was to reveal the web of shame and secrecy that restricts us from intimacy with others. After reading this story, I'd like to offer you an opportunity to take a *coaching class* with me:

1) To discuss more in depth the topics in this book;

2) To have a safe place to share *your* story;

3) To unearth some of the cultural lies, self-limiting beliefs, and destructive behaviors;

4) To come to a place of moving forward with *your* healing.

Couching Classes will be conducted either individually or in a small group setting.

Please contact me through my webpage www.sallybetters.com or email me at info@sallybetters.com. A portion of the proceeds from each book and coaching classes will be donated to organizations which fight human trafficking.

NOTES

CHAPTER 1   THE SECRETS

1.   "Quotes by Corrie Ten Boom, The Hiding Place," https://www.goodreads.com accessed, March 28, 2018.

CHAPTER 2   GOD'S HAND OF PROTECTION

1.   Max Lucado, https://www.christianquotes.info/ top-quotes, accessed April 6, 2018.
2.   Iranian Revolution, http://en.wikipedia.org/ wikiIranian_Revolution, accessed April 17, 2018.

CHAPTER 3   THE UGLY HEAD OF MY LEARNING DISABILITY ERUPTS

1.   Agatha Christie, www.brainprick. com/10-successful-and-famous-people-wh o-had-dyslexia, accessed May 12,2018.
2.   Villines, Zawn. *What is Dyslexia in Adults,* www. medicalnewstoday.com/articles/319972.php, accessed May 15, 2018

CHAPTER 5   SIGNS OF CHANGE

1. Bancroft, Lundy, (2002) Why Does He Do That? New York, New York, Penguin Publishing Group

CHAPTER 6   THE UNVEILING

1. "Inspirational Quotes," https://eternallifeministries. org/quotes.htm, accessed May 20, 2018.
2. Ann Voskamp Blog post, retrieved from: https:// www.goodreads.com/author/show/1890390. annvoskamp's blog

CHAPTER 7   THE MIRACLES

1. "Grace Quotes," https://gracequotes.org/author-quote/ john-newton, accessed May 23, 2018.

CHAPTER 8   RESTORATION AND HEALING

1. "Christianquotes," https://www.christianquotes.info/... francis-frangipane-quotes, accessed May 25, 2018.
2. Eldridge, Stasi. (2005) *Captivating*, Nashville, Tennessee, Nelson Books.

CHAPTER 9   RECOGNIZING THE LOSS

1. Brainyquotes, https://www.brainyquote.com/quotes/ norman_cousins_121747, accessed May 28, 2018.
2. Brown, Dr. Brene'. (2012) *Daring Greatly, How the Courage to Be Vulnerable Transforms the Way We Live, Love, Parent, and Lead*, New York, New York, Penguin Random House.
3. Allender, Dr. Dan. (1990) *The Wounded Heart – Hope for Adult Victims of Childhood Sexual Abuse*, Colorado Springs, NavPress.
4. "What is The Grief Recovery Method Support Group," https://www.griefrecoverymethod.com/ grief-support-groups , accessed May 20, 2018

CHAPTER 11   ENCOURAGEMENT FOR EACH DAY

1. AZQuotes, www.azqquotes.com >Authors>Charles Spurgeon
2. Young, Sarah. (2011) *Jesus Calling – Enjoying Peace in His Presence*, Nashville, Tennessee, Thomas Nelson.

CHAPTER 12   BEING THE HANDS AND FEET

1. AZQuotes, www.azquotes.com/author/8805-C_S_Lewis
2. "Images of who chart lifetime impact of child sexual abuse," www.bing.com/images, Source: WHO, accessed May 28, 2018.
3. National Sexual Assault Hotline. https://hotline.rainn.org/online/, accessed May 20, 2018.
4. "Reading is for Everyone," https://www.readinghorizons.com/, accessed May 21, 2018.
5. Feister, L. (2012) Don't "DYS" our kids: Dyslexia and the quest for grade level Reading Proficiency, National Center for Learning Disabilities (2011) The State of Learning Disabilities, accessed May 18, 2018.
6. Flanders, Nancy. *Live Action*, November 28, 2014, https://www.liveaction.org/news/author/nancy/page/59/, accessed May 25, 2018
7. "Abortion worker has nightmares after counting fetal…" www.clinicquotes.com/abortion-worker-has-nightmares-after-counting, accessed May 29, 2018.
8. Masse, Sydna. (2013) *Her Choice to Heal: finding Spiritual and emotional peace after abortion*, Fayetteville, Arkansas, Ramah International, Inc., www.hearchoicetoheal.com
9. "U.S. Women Who Have Abortions," https://www.guttmacher.org/, accessed May 25, 2018.

10. VandePol, Susan. (2015) *Life after breath*, New York, Morgan James Publishing., www.mattersoflifeandbreath.com

11. "Arthur Ashe Quotes About Life, Sports, and Success," https://everydaypowerblog.com/arthur-ashe-quotes-2, accessed May 26, 2018.

12. Roosevelt's "The Man in the Arena", https://www.mentalfloss.com/article/63390/roosevelts-man-arena, accessed May 29, 2018.

13. 13. AZQuotes, www.azquote.com/author/14530-Mother_Teresa, accessed May 23, 2018

CHAPTER 13   EYES WIDE OPEN

1. Quote by William Wilberforce, https://www.goodreads.com/quotes/61653-you-may-ch oose-to-look-the-other-way-but-you, accessed, June 2, 2018.

ABOUT THE AUTHOR

Sally Betters is an entrepreneur at heart with diverse experience in small business ownership and community involvement. She has owned and operated a professional tutorial services business, More than Words, for over fifteen years. She is passionate about her work with individuals who struggle with learning differences. Witnessing both incremental and drastic improvement in her students' self-esteem and academic growth is rewarding and fulfilling. Additionally, she has coached women, both young and old, in various levels of emotional, mental and spiritual development on the topics contained within this book. Others are attracted to her leadership in group environments because of her deep compassion, knowledge base and willingness to work with diverse groups.

As a Certified Professional Tutor specializing in children and adults with Dyslexia, Dysgraphia and Attention Deficit Disorder. Sally Betters speaks to parent groups educating them on research-based systems. She has significantly impacted numerous students and their families with her expertise.

As an advocate on the effects of post abortion on women, Sally Betters has been invited to speak to churches, pastors, and community groups. She has been a volunteer, a case manager, and a staff member with the Post Abortion Counseling Program for the Santa Clarita Valley Pregnancy Center. In addition, she has served as a founding Board Member of the Vine Pregnancy Center in her local mountain community.

Sally Betters currently resides in Southern California with her husband, who is her soul mate. Together they have four adult children and four beautiful granddaughters.

To contact Sally, for information on booking her to speak at your event, visit her website at www.sallybetters.com. If you're interested in personal coaching you can email her at info@ sallybetters.com.

Continue your experience
with *From Crisis to Compassion*

I extend a hand to you to carry forward your experience with *From Crisis to Compassion* at my website: www.sallybetters.com.

- *Reactions and revelations about the book.*

- *How did it impact you?*

- *Communicate with the author.*

- *Order additional copies for those who will be impacted by it.*

For information about having the author speak to your organization or group, please contact Sally Betters at info@ sallybetters.com.

CPSIA information can be obtained
at www.ICGtesting.com
Printed in the USA
FSHW02n1437110918